Katarzyna Hano

Jury Decision Making and Social Network Analysis

Katarzyna Hano

Jury Decision Making and Social Network Analysis

VDM Verlag Dr. Müller

Imprint

Bibliographic information by the German National Library: The German National Library lists this publication at the German National Bibliography; detailed bibliographic information is available on the Internet at http://dnb.d-nb.de.

Any brand names and product names mentioned in this book are subject to trademark, brand or patent protection and are trademarks or registered trademarks of their respective holders. The use of brand names, product names, common names, trade names, product descriptions etc. even without a particular marking in this works is in no way to be construed to mean that such names may be regarded as unrestricted in respect of trademark and brand protection legislation and could thus be used by anyone.

Cover image: www.purestockx.com

Publisher:
VDM Verlag Dr. Müller Aktiengesellschaft & Co. KG
Dudweiler Landstr. 125 a, 66123 Saarbrücken, Germany
Phone +49 681 9100-698, Fax +49 681 9100-988, Email: info@vdm-verlag.de

Produced in USA and UK by:
Lightning Source Inc., La Vergne, Tennessee, USA
Lightning Source UK Ltd., Milton Keynes, UK
BookSurge LLC, 5341 Dorchester Road, Suite 16, North Charleston, SC 29418, USA

ISBN: 978-3-8364-3827-8

Abstract

In this thesis I combine the social network analysis approach with the traditional experimental approach to study the phenomena of jury decision-making. I examine whether with each trial a social network is formed. The jurors, the two teams of lawyers, as well as the accused and the judge, all form a social network with cliques and leaders. This division of individuals into specific cliques, along with the lawyers' performance in court, is hypothesized to have a significant impact on the jury's verdict.

Thus, by specifically studying the lawyers' engagement and disengagement on the jurors during a trial and the impact this has on the verdict, as well as understanding the structure of the social network that the individual jurors create, I hope to shed light on some of the influences that are key in delivering the verdict. In addition, this pioneering study may lead to significant policy changes in the future.

Acknowledgements

I would like to thank Dr. Peter Carrington, Dr. Steve Spencer, and Dr. Fred Desroches for their help, strong belief in this project, and their patience.

I would also like to thank Ashley B. and Alex who not only recruited actors for the mock trial, but staged managed and directed the production. Without their help and expertise I would not have been able to finish this project so quickly and efficiently.

Many thanks to all the actors who volunteered their time to memorize lines and come to rehearsals in order to help me out. All of you were amazing and the proof lies in the results of my thesis.

Many thanks to Scott Charles and his team in the Audio-Visual Department, who not only videotaped the mock trials, but also the study, and spent many hours editing the tapes. Without your expertise I would not have a study.

Thank you to my two coders for doing an excellent job at observing participants and coding their interactions.

A very big thank you to Gwen Schell for the editing of my work. Thank you for spending many hours reading and rereading my work, correcting it, and giving me suggestions and pointing out my weaknesses. You have been with this project from the start, and I know that by now you know my work as well as I do, and yet you are still able to look at and make it even better. Your help over the last years will never be forgotten, since it was so incredible.

Many thanks to the Office for Persons with Disabilities, and the RITT team, who helped me with research, transcribed articles, and Brailed them. Your professionalism, expertise, and understanding made my work not only much easier, but devoid of stress, and very speedy.

Lastly, thank you to my friends and family for their patience, sympathetic ears, support, and for sharing my success and my joys along the way. Without all of you, I would not be where I am today, or who I am today.

Dedication

To Dr. Jim Curtis, who was not only a wonderful person and a great Sociologist, but also very enthusiastic about my project. Unfortunately, he was unable to see the finished product. His suggestions and memory will always be a part of this work.

Table of Contents

List of Tables

List of Figures

1   Introduction

Jury trials are used in North American society. Their primary purpose is to convict the guilty and acquit the innocent. The paramount question arises: how does this group of people chosen from the general population make these decisions? Can this group of people make accurate decisions to convict the guilty while acquitting the innocent? Literature shows there are many factors that come to play significant roles in the jury's verdict. Most of these factors have very little to do with the evidence presented to the jury. The goal of this paper is to describe the factors that play an important role in jury decision-making. More importantly, however, the impact of lawyers' approaches to the presentation of the case on the jurors' decision will be discussed.

The influence of lawyers on jurors while they form invisible connections has not been studied by researchers who use Social Network Analysis. Previous studies have shown how the lawyers' emotional engagement and interaction with the jurors, versus no interaction with jurors at all, influences the jurors' decision. However, this form of interaction has not been examined with the use of social network analysis.

This paper will begin by examining the process of jury selection and how social network analysis can be applied to represent this newly formed social structure. Second, evidence will be presented as to how the jurors view, act, and react during the trial. Third, the deliberation process will be described, and how jurors' positions within this newly formed network will impact the verdict. Lastly, the influence of the lawyers on the jurors' decision will be examined.

1.1 Social Network Analysis and Jury Selection

Once the lawyers choose the jury, which is made up of 12 individuals from the general population, initially there is nothing but the trial and the accused connecting the 12 people together. Social network analysis defines this as a STAR. This means that the accused has a relationship with these 12 individuals; however, they do not have a relationship with each other at this point (Scott, 2000, p.10). The accused has chosen to take steps in his/her life that have led him/her to the upcoming trial. The behaviour of the accused has led the lawyers to choose a group of citizens to whom the accused, through the help of his/her lawyers, will communicate the series of events. The relationship that the accused has thus created with the 12 jury members is a channel through which information is going to flow. Many tools that have their basis in persuasion will be used to communicate to the jury the accused's story of events (Scott, 2000). Therefore, even though the 12 individuals who form the jury may never meet the accused or form inter-personal relationships with him/her, the trial will open channels through which information will pass. Thus, it is the accused who is the central character of the star, since the accused is strongly motivated to formulate an invisible tie with the 12 jurors (Scott, 2000, p.10).

Figure 1

Star Diagram

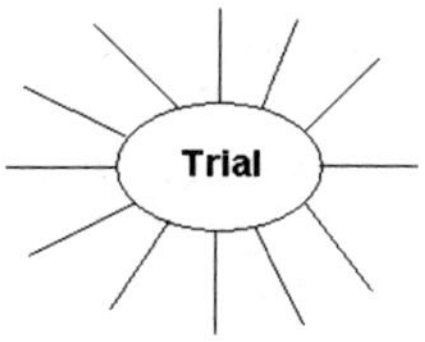

If it were not for the accused, the 12 individual jury members would not have come together to create an understanding and make sense of the events. This understanding could not be acquired without the flow of information from the accused to the group of jurors.

As the trial begins and progresses, the channels and ties between the accused and the jurors are going to become stronger; the ties will also strengthen between the jurors themselves. In addition, this relationship will be reciprocal. As the jurors hear the evidence, through their facial expressions, they will reciprocate the communication. When the lawyers are selecting the 12 members of the jury, they look for favorable attitudes; that is, attitudes that are similar to those of the accused. For example, in a friendship relationship person A that likes person B not only has a positive connection with that person, but also a similar attitude (Scott, 2000, p. 10). The same concept can be applied here. Those individual jurors who hold similar attitudes to the accused, or have a friend similar to the accused, will identify with that person. This relationship is established by asking the jurors questions that pertain to the case at hand. The lawyers look for personal characteristics in the jurors that reflect those of the accused, so that if the two were to meet, the basis for an interpersonal relationship would be there.

This newly formed social group exists in a social space and connects the group with its surrounding environment. This environment is perceived by group members and its meaning is constructed by group members on the basis of its context. The jury creates an environment, which is an element within the larger social field (Scott, 2000, p.11). Each one of the jurors is a member of a social class, holds a certain political view, and is a member within many other social groups, such as church or recreation. All of these factors are important, as they form the jurors' attitudes and will have an impact on the individual's position within this network. They will influence whether the individual will become a leader or follower in the group, and inadvertently impact the decision. In addition, it will have an impact on being chosen as a juror, since the accused's lawyer will look for jurors who hold congruent attitudes with the accused. Similarly, the prosecution will look for previously established attitudes that would be congruent with their own attitudes, outlook, and the current case.

The position of the accused within society will also play a role in jury selection. For instance, an accused member of the upper class has the financial resources to hire experts or consultants, which can lead to a greater chance of being found not guilty rather than guilty. This individual would have the financial resources to hire jury experts to advise his/her lawyers as to what characteristics they should look for in a jury, in order to receive the desired verdict (Hans & Vidmar, 1986, Thagard, 2003). This was clearly demonstrated in the O.J. Simpson murder trial. Simpson's lawyers hired a team of jury consultants who conducted analyses, that showed which individuals would make favorable jurors.

The analysis showed that 20% of the potential juror sample believed Simpson to be innocent, while 50% did not want to believe Simpson was guilty (Thagard, 2003). Further analysis showed that middle-class black women were Simpson's largest supporters; Simpson's jury was composed of eight middle-aged black women who wanted Simpson acquitted. With this kind of jury composition, it should not be surprising that the verdict was "not guilty" (Thagard, 2003). Furthermore, in-depth analysis showed that 75% of the black population in Los Angeles County believed the police framed Simpson. It is believed that personal experience and social position within the larger white social structure impacted on the attitudes of the black population. It is possible that through their networking, black individuals of Los Angeles heard of or observed many cases in which the police framed black people (Thagard, 2003). It is reasonable to believe that many jurors were emotionally biased toward Simpson since they had made prior positive connections with him (Thagard, 2003).

Even though Simpson's trial may have begun with an emotional bias to acquit him, it was not the only factor that determined the verdict. There were the interactions between the jurors, as well as the explanations of what happened that were presented by both teams of the defense and prosecution, that played a significant role (Thagard, 2003). Since Simpson's trial was widely publicized and evidence has already shown that many black individuals were previously pro-Simpson, it could be said that the spectators who attended Simpson's trial may have impacted the jurors. This is especially true if they were similar to the composition of the jury. Unfortunately, research was not conducted in

5

this area to shed more light on this subject. As a result, it can only be speculated that the spectators' reactions had an impact on the jurors' decision, but it is neither confirmed nor denied. Moreover, few trials are publicized in the same manner that the Simpson trial. Individuals are accused of murder and stand trial every day, but the public does not hear of the accused as they did of Simpson's trial. Thus, it is important to keep in mind that the O.J. Simpson trial may not be representative of all murder cases.

This idea of preconceived notions of innocence or guilt violates one of the core assumptions that juries appear in court with a "blank slate" and are not influenced by life experiences and pretrial publicity. Ideally, those jurors who hold prejudicial attitudes will be dismissed from jury duty (Kassin & Wrightsman, 1988). Since each lawyer's team is looking for individuals that would favour their client, this ideal may be violated. Indeed, before the trial even begins, a specific point of view will be represented. However, since the two opposing teams (prosecution versus the defence team) have a say in who will become a juror or not, there will be some viewpoint differences.

When the newly formed jury of 12 strangers comes together, they will form some negative connections and some positive connections. The jury quickly forms a network within which there are subgroups, or cliques, with both positive and negative connections. Those individuals who hold similar attitudes will form positive connections, while those who hold different attitudes will have negative connections with them, but form a subgroup among themselves (Scott, 2000, p.12). These cliques will have a very powerful influence on the verdict during the deliberation process of the trial. Since these individuals are going to become emotionally close to each other, they will respond in a congruent fashion, which may have a significant impact on the verdict (Scott, 2000).

Although there may be a strain between subgroups, within groups there will be a balance of attitudes and opinions (Scott, 2000).

As the trial progresses, the jurors will get to know one another and their connections will strengthen, especially since they cannot discuss the trial until the time of deliberation. They will learn each other's attitudes and opinions on a variety of issues. Many of the jurors' ideas and opinions on a variety of social issues may overlap with others in adjacent cliques. Jury membership in a clique is not exclusive; each jury member can belong to different cliques. Even though there may be different cliques among the 12 jury members, the 12 as a group compose the core of the network and interact with one another most often (Scott, 2000, p.22). The accused and the lawyers comprise the primary circle of the network. These individuals interact with the core, the jury, but do not share the same level of intimacy (Scott, 2000, p.22). The lawyers are strongly motivated to communicate to the jurors the case of the accused and will form a tie or reciprocal relationship. Even though their roles as lawyers place them in the primary circle, they use many types of communication sources to create a bond with the jurors. Once again that relationship will not to be a typical relationship where individuals communicate with one another on a regular basis. However, similar to a typical relationship, the messages that jurors will send to the members of the primary circle will be through invisible channels and may take the form of facial reactions. This is referred to as emotional contagion (Thagard, 2004). When the jurors hear evidence from the lawyers, they have emotional reactions that are visible to others and are universal in meaning. Similar to the spread of a contagious disease, those emotions are spread from one juror to the other. For instance, when one juror smiles in response to the evidence,

7

and another juror looks at him/her, he/she will pick up on that emotion and smile as well. This has major implications, as the jurors do not need verbal communication to understand others' feelings, opinions, and positions on an issue. They can easily read the feelings and opinions of the spectators, lawyers, as well as everybody else's in the courtroom. This is possible only because the emotions diffuse among the individuals in the network (Thagard, 2004). The following are Thagard's propositions of the three stages as to how this occurs:

> Proposition 1. In conversation, people tend automatically and continuously to mimic and synchronize their movements with the facial expressions, voices, postures, movements, and instrumental behavior of others.

> Proposition 2. Subjective emotional experiences are affected, moment to moment, by the activation and/or feedback from such mimicry.

> Proposition 3. Given propositions 1 and 2, people tend to "catch" others' emotions, moment to moment (2004, pp.10-11).

This means that jurors, through non-verbal communication, very clearly communicate to the lawyers their feelings and opinions. This communication would be as clear as if the lawyers and the jury had conducted regular discussions and had interpersonal interactions.

In addition to the jury clique, each team of lawyers and their experts will form a clique. Within each team's clique, there will be a balance of attitudes and opinions, although between the cliques there may be a strain. Last, but not least, there is the secondary circle, which is composed of reporters, spectators and individuals/groups that infrequently connect with the core (Scott, 2000, p.22). These individuals who compose the secondary circle have put in place similar channels that those from the primary circle have, which lead to the core.

Figure 2

Newly-Formed Network

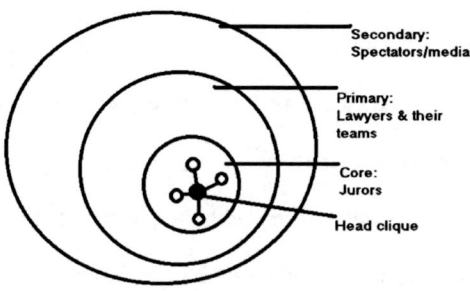

However, unlike the members of the primary circle, they may not use them as often; that is, they may be present, but passive. When they feel the need to inform the core of their beliefs, they will use the established channels to pass the message. By voicing their ideas they will send the message to the core, which in turn will be received and reciprocated. The reciprocation may take different forms depending on the nature of the tie with that specific group of spectators. Thus, even though the spectators and the jurors may never meet, they will have built a relationship on the basis of mutual goals and motivations. These goals are to understand the information presented to them, and on those bases deliver a quick and unanimous verdict.

It is perceived that for a group to reach a unanimous decision, both verbal and nonverbal interaction is equally used. The non-verbal interaction is most often shown through emotional expressions (Thagard, 2004). Thus, the jury will collect the nonverbal emotional expressions from the spectators and use them in reaching the verdict. For example, if the spectators are scowling or sneering when they hear evidence, the jurors will know exactly what that group thinks and feels, and what their stand on the issue is (Thagard, 2004).

Ideally, the judge is not a member of any circle; the judges' role can be seen as a mediator (Scott, 2000). Since the judge is the one who is connected to all network members, he/she must oversee and keep the whole network in balance (Scott, 2000). Now that the jury is selected and the network is in place, it is time to move on to the trial.

1.2   Trial and Social Network Analysis

At the beginning of the trial, lawyers with their teams of experts present their story of the events, each trying to present the evidence in such a way as to convince the jury that their story is the true version. While the jury is listening to the lawyers, witnesses, etc., they are strengthening their connections between the core cliques and the primary circle. Similar to how the connections have been formed within each clique, some will be positive and others will be negative. Some jury members will identify with some of the lawyers and witnesses, whereas others will not. These connections made during the trial, are going to become vital during deliberations, upon which the verdict will be based (Scott, 2000; Kassin & Wrightsman, 1988). For example, if the jury really forms positive connections and identifies with the accused, then the verdict may be "not guilty". This would be especially true when the spectators react to the evidence of the defence in a positive way, and through the nature of their reaction convey to the jury their stand on the issue.

10

There are some key factors that the jury uses to evaluate the witnesses and form

the positive or negative connection. During the trial the jury learns about the background

of the witnesses, which influences their decision on whether to believe that person is

trustworthy or not. This will be determined based on how the lawyers communicate to the

jury the information about the witnesses. Another factor is the witnesses' motivation to

testify. The question that naturally comes to mind is: "what is in it for them?" The story

needs to make sense, both physically and psychologically. The jury will turn to their

personal experiences and socially constructed knowledge to evaluate the witnesses

(Kassin & Wrightsman, 1988).

Since both teams of lawyers are strongly motivated to win the case, they bring

expert witnesses to help them make the case stronger. Many of these experts use very

scientific terminology that to laypersons or non-scientists sounds impressive, even when

its methodology is flawed. Jurors who hear such testimony, unless they have formal

scientific training, are impressed by the testimony and may make decisions based on

flawed evidence (Bull Kovera, Russano, & McAuliff, 2002). Kovera et al., (2002)

conducted a series of studies to evaluate the jurors' ability to identify problems with

expert testimony. The findings of their studies show that jurors may be unable to

recognize problems in the evidence presented by experts. Based on their research

findings, the researchers concluded that unless the jurors receive assistance in helping

them identify flaws in the experts' testimony, they lack the necessary skills to do the

evaluation themselves (Bull Kovera et al., 2002; Worthington, Stallard, Price, & Goss,

2002). These researchers also studied the judges' ability to identify flawed testimony and

found that, similar to the jurors, judges were unable to recognize flaws in scientific expert testimony (Bull Kovera, et al., 2002). Since the judges are unable to recognize the flaws, they are unable to prevent the testimony from being presented in court. As a result, jurors may be making decisions based on flawed information. Not only that, they may turn to spectators for help in evaluating the evidence. By observing the reaction of the spectators, jurors may take hints and later use those hints to make the decision as to whether the person is guilty or not. Since limited research has been conducted in this area, this idea is only speculation. What is known is that cross-examination does not correct the flaws like it is believed (Bull Kovera et al., 2002). During cross-examination, it is believed that lawyers ask questions that deal with the methodology that the expert has presented. The intention of the questioning is to bring out different flaws in the methodology. Since the expert testimony appears solid to all involved in the trial to begin with, cross-examination will be unable to bring those flaws to the jurors' attention.

Studies demonstrate that when the testimony presented to the jurors becomes overly complicated and difficult to understand and comprehend, they focus on unrelated aspects of the witness to make a judgment (Rosenthal, 1983; Worthington, et al., 2002). Jurors acquire much of their information on a subject from the media, and bring that point of view into the courtroom. In the courtroom, they spend much time listening to testimony that they cannot understand; it would not be surprising that the jurors turn to spectators for help. If the media representatives are part of the spectators that previously have informed the jurors on the subject, those jurors may follow their lead in understanding the case, since they already have made a positive connection with these groups or individuals. These groups or individuals would previously have created a very atypical relationship that possesses the same attributes of a typical interpersonal relationship. For example, through watching the programs that are created by the group

or individual there would be silent interaction. The jurors would have seen the previous

context in which the group or individual presented their ideas. That presentation will

deliver the message to the jury. That is, the content of the message would contain their

attitudes and opinions. Thus, seeing that group or individual in court would bring forth to

jurors' minds those attitudes and opinions. Therefore, even though the jury members may

never meet the individual members of the spectators, they would know their attitudes and

opinions. Consequently, one does not need to have met a person and have a one-on-one

interaction with the person to know their attitudes, opinions, and have formed a

trustworthy relationship. These relationships have not been studied by social network

analysis, and thus are only theoretical speculations that need to be tested.

Researchers have also found that many of the jurors use the hindsight bias when

making their decisions and not the evidence presented in court. Hindsight bias is defined

as, "a person's tendency to judge past decisions in light of one's current knowledge of the

outcome" (Worthington et al., 2002, p.155). The researchers found that the media

presented information about a case, which the jurors have seen. As a result, during the

trial the jurors turned to the media portrayal of the case to make judgments (Worthington

et al., 2002). The researchers used the case of the dangers of silicon breast implants. The

media presented health problems that could be caused by silicon breast implants, and

many individuals were educated on the issue through watching or reading media reports.

Therefore, when those individuals were selected to be jurors, they brought that

knowledge with them into the courtroom. Since they did not understand the evidence in

court they relied on their prior knowledge to make the decision (Worthington et al.,

13

2002). They also relied on the witnesses' appearance and paralanguage, and not on the testimony (Rosenthal, 1983; Worthington et al., 2002). Jurors therefore use the connections that they have with other networks in society to strengthen or weaken a connection within this trial network. They are not "blank slates," like it is ideally assumed. These are examples of how trustworthy relationships can be built without interpersonal interaction. Even though these relationships have been built and are silent, they are very much alive and influential.

Putting aside witnesses' testimony and their impact on the strength and type of the connection with the jury, attractiveness also has an impact in the courtroom. The attractiveness of lawyers, the accused, witnesses, etc., will play a major role in determining how the jury will react. Attractiveness has nothing to do with the innocence or guilt of the accused, yet it will play a significant role in the verdict (Kassin & Wrightsman, 1988). Our society has preconceived notions of attractiveness that influence how individuals see others and are influenced by them. On the surface, people will say things such as: "do not judge a book by its cover", but in reality, how others are viewed will very much depend on their physical attractiveness (Kassin & Wrightsman, 1988, p. 100). Attractive people are portrayed in our society as being more honest, talented, warm, intelligent, etc., than those who are less attractive (Kassin & Wrightsman, 1988). Since jurors are members of a society that propagates these views, they are affected by them in the courtroom. Mock jury studies show that it pays to look good. (Kassin & Wrightsman, 1988).

In a study that was conducted in Pennsylvania, court researchers rated the physical attractiveness of 74 male criminal defendants on a seven-point scale. Their results showed that the more attractive the defendant, the lighter the sentence (Kassin & Wrightsman, 1988). This is very significant since the jury will be attracted to some individuals, which will strengthen their connection. Whichever team a jury clique is attracted to (i.e. defense versus prosecution) may have a big impact. The jury will like those people, identify with them, and become emotionally attached. As a result, they will not base their judgments on the evidence, but rather on their emotions. By discussing the attractiveness of the members within the primary circle, the cliques would be influenced by their group members and adopt a similar attitude in order to maintain the balance within the group (Scott, 2000). The individuals would not be breaking any rules about not discussing the trial if they were to discuss attractiveness.

Hobbs (2003) discusses the impression management that lawyers use in the courtroom to persuade the jurors. She describes the different techniques that lawyers use in order to make positive connections with the jurors. Hobbs used segments of prosecutors' rebuttal arguments from a criminal trial to illustrate her point. A trial can be viewed as a dramatic performance in which lawyers play leading roles while jurors, who play the role of an audience, evaluate the content of the presentation, as well as the key players. Thus, when lawyers present their cases it is their personalities, demeanors, and appearance that are on trial (Hobbs, 2003). Lawyers, similar to politicians, strive to win the votes of jurors, and consequently they play to the audience. They recognize that in order to win a juror's vote, a positive connection needs to be made. Since jurors tend to identify with those they like, establishing a shared identity with the jurors is the key to obtaining their trust. Lawyers' careful choice of language, dress and style are the factors that will make connections with jurors. For instance, if a lawyer uses language that the

15

jury has a hard time understanding, does not make eye contact with the jurors, and wears brown, jurors most likely will not make positive connections with them (Hobbs, 2003). The analysis shows that choice of blue represents sincerity, red represents power, and brown was, overall, not a good choice (Hobbs, 2003). Young female lawyers may also want to wear glasses, since the spectacles will make them appear more mature and intelligent (Hobbs, 2003). The other important aspects that would make connections with jurors are spontaneity and cultural references. For instance, a lawyer who appears to be spontaneous in that she speaks freely without looking at her notes, signals to the jurors friendliness and informality, as her speech flows like a conversation and not like a lecture (Hobbs, 2003).

Referring to the culture of the jurors will also help establish a positive connection with the jurors (Hobbs, 2003). For example, a black lawyer, who is presenting a case to a mostly black jury and uses specific terms used by that group, will form a positive affiliation with that group (Hobbs, 2003). This has significant implications since it is the lawyers' acting ability that may play a more important role in the jurors' decision, than the evidence presented. Since spectators would view the same performance as the jurors, their reactions may be congruent with the jurors' position and it may confirm and reinforce their opinions. Research needs to be conducted to test this.

Feelings of sympathy toward the victim may play a large role in the verdict as well. For instance, if the victim is mentally disabled and claims that he/she has been harmed, the jury will sympathize with that victim. The general consensus in our society is that these individuals are more vulnerable and more easily exploited. In a mock jury trial 160 men and women viewed a videotape of a trial where the victim was sexually assaulted. However, one group saw the victim as being mentally disabled, whereas the other group saw the individual as mentally and physically healthy. The results showed that jurors were more likely to return a guilty verdict when the victim was mentally disabled than when the victim was not (Bottoms, Nysse-Carris, Harris, & Tyda, 2003). Once again this illustrates that jurors do not come into a trial with a clean slate. They were also more confident in their verdict, which suggests more balance and cohesion amongst the cliques (Scott, 2000). This also means that during the trial the jury did not necessarily focus on the evidence, but turned to their emotions and preexisting influences to reach their decision.

All of the above examples have been tested separately, which means that each team of researchers only looked at only one small aspect at a time. Together, all of these small parts build the network and establish different types of connections. By applying social network analysis one can study all of these concepts and influences simultaneously. The benefits are numerous. First, the researchers would look at the whole, and not just at different parts of the whole. This could be comparable to looking at a map, in which an individual would only study a small part of the map and not the whole. The small part would present a solution to a single problem, but the whole would shed light on other possibilities, connections, and influences. Each study sheds light on a small part, but social network analysis would provide the complete picture. It would include each part and that part's connection and association with the other parts within this network. By looking at the trial as a whole, each part's role would be examined, and their interactions that may have escaped the notice of other researchers, would be identified and explained

Throughout the trial, the jury listens to an overwhelming amount of information. Legally, they cannot discuss this information after they have heard it, but must wait until it is time to deliberate. It should therefore not be surprising that the jury spends the time after court talking about themselves, their lives and making the connections between each other stronger. These subgroups or cliques that the jury divided themselves into not only provides alliances among individuals, but also provides the support needed during deliberations (Hans & Vidmar, 1986).

1.3   Deliberations

Once the trial is complete, the jury is ready to deliberate and decide if the accused is guilty or not guilty. Before deliberations begin, the jury needs to elect a leader known as the foreman or forewoman. At this point in the trial, the jury has spent much time together, so this normally takes only a few minutes. While the jury was getting to know each other during the trial, natural leaders emerged. Therefore, the procedure of choosing a foreman/forewoman does not take long. There are different ways by which an individual is chosen. He/she is mostly nominated by the group and asked to be the leader. The people that nominate the foreman/forewoman are the members of that person's clique and have made alliances with them during the trial (Hans & Vidmar, 1986). This process may appear unstructured, but in fact it is very structured and reflects the structure in society at large. For example, those individuals who are leaders within their social networks outside the courtroom will be the individuals who are selected to be leaders in the jury room (Hans & Vidmar, 1986). These individuals tend to occupy a high status in society, have a higher education, are well-connected in a general social network, and/or have previous jury experience, and so are believed to be experts in the field (Hans &

Vidmar, 1986; Scott, 2000). Studies of mock jury trials have shown that those individuals who sit at the head of the table and speak first during deliberations are the ones chosen to be the foreman/forewoman. The results of these studies also show that high status individuals are most likely to sit at the head of the table and speak first during deliberations (Hans & Vidmar, 1986). It does not mean that this will happen in every single trial, but in most trials it is the norm. This is another example of how individual connections within society are important to jury decision-making.

The idea behind jury deliberation is to finally discuss the case, ask questions and scrutinize one's own view. This is achieved through an exchange of information, otherwise known as diffusion (Kassin & Wrightsman, 1988; Scott, 2000). Diffusion, in social network analysis, refers to the passage of information from one member to another (Scott, 2000). In the jury room, the jurors are asked to share their views, ideas, and perceptions of the trial with one another. Even though all the jurors have seen and experienced the same trial, they may not have understood some evidence in the same way as other jurors. During deliberations, they pass on information about the trial (Kassin & Wrightsman, 1988). Every juror is motivated by the same goal: they all want to reach a verdict quickly and return to their daily lives. Since the motivation is high, an individual juror will not need to go through many links within the social network of the jury to obtain the information they are seeking (Scott, 2000). Once the discussion begins, it picks up speed and momentum. The leaders present their ideas, while others challenge or explain them; very quickly the group becomes absorbed and involved. In social network analysis, this is referred to as snowballing (Kassin & Wrightsman 1988; Scott, 2000).

Leaders possess much power, support and have many alliances. If they see the accused in a certain light and present their point of view to the jury members, others will listen and follow by the very nature of their position in the network. Studies of mock juries show that once one individual presents a certain point of view to the group, the group will follow that pattern of thinking (Hans & Vidmar, 1986). Since the leader is well-connected within the group, it is not going to be hard to have other members see the leader's point of view. At times the leader and his followers are so passionate about their position, that pressure is applied to have the other jurors agree; this may occur through verbal abuse or threats (Hans & Vidmar, 1986). Some jurors feel too intimidated and fearful to present their point of view, and as a result follow the leader. Those individuals would rather be liked by others than rejected (Kassin &Wrightsman, 1988).

One of the core assumptions behind deliberations is that during the time when jurors are heavily involved in discussions of the case, the discussion will fill the gaps in jurors' memories. As a result, the verdict will be based on accurate and precise information (Prechard & Keenan, 2002). However, studies show that deliberations only slightly improve jurors' memories, because the jurors felt they were not forgetting key information, and consequently did not think that their memories needed to improve (Prichard & Keenan, 2002). The leaders were more likely to be inaccurate in their memories (Prichard & Keenan, 2002). The leaders were confident in the correctness of their memories, whereas those who may have had better recollection than the leaders, were not confident enough in their memory and, as a result, were able to be persuaded (Prichard & Keenan, 2002). Collective memory of the jurors is key to reaching a correct verdict. Since trials can take a long time, during which time discussion may not take place, much evidence may be forgotten. Jurors are presented with so much information, and at times are asked to disregard some pieces but remember others, that they are unable to remember it all (Kassin & Wrightsman, 1988). People usually remember information, but not its source. It would be comparable to asking students to only use lecture material on the test and disregard the text. This is precisely what the jury is asked to do. At some point during the trial, the jury will be asked to disregard some evidence but later, while they are deliberating, they may not remember that a specific point was not to be considered (Kassin & Wrightsman, 1988). The implications are profound, since the verdict may be based on information and evidence that was not to be used. If this is the case, how the spectators react to evidence may become very memorable, even when it has nothing to do with the trial. In addition, if the evidence was presented by a lawyer who had already made a positive connection with the jury, the innocence or guilt of the accused could possibly become irrelevant.

All these issues aside, the jury experiences much pressure from the secondary circle. Seeing their desired verdict become the verdict that the jury delivers drives these individuals. They are very motivated to communicate to the jury their opinions and views. Their opinions diffuse through different links until it reaches the jury. The jury takes hints from the media, spectators, and their families, as well as from the important leaders in their private lives. They want to make the right decision, however, what the public thinks and feels is very close to jurors' hearts (Kassin & Wrightsman 1988). Since the jury will need to return to their social networks once the trial is over, they do not want to sever the connections that they have in these networks. Even though they may not fully believe that the accused is innocent or guilty, they may deliver the desired verdict, not necessarily the true verdict (Scott, 2000; Kassin & Wrightsman, 1988). Most media

sources such as television, Internet, and newspapers, to mention only a few, present

reports of criminal cases. In many cases the reports contain details as to what occurred.

Since most members in today's society have access to those reports before a trial even

begins, potential jurors have the opportunity to form their opinions (Constitutional Rights

Foundation, 2000). The potential jurors not only form their own opinions before the trial

begins, but members of their network are able to present their views and opinions as well.

Studies show that in heavily publicized criminal cases, jurors become prejudiced before

the trial begins, and as a result base their verdicts on the public opinion and not on the

evidence presented to them during the trial (Constitutional Rights Foundation, 2000).

Many of the reporters who report about the cases to the public before the trial, appear in

court as spectators and may impact the jurors (Constitutional Rights Foundation, 2000).

This was evidenced during the trial of Sam Sheppard, who was a wealthy

Cleveland doctor, on trial for murdering his wife. All through his trial the press,

cameramen and photographers interfered in the proceedings. Since the judge did very

little to stop the press, jurors were not only exposed to pretrial publicity, but to the very

clear opinions of the press during the trial. It should not be surprising that Sheppard was

convicted (Constitutional Rights Foundation, 2000). Sheppard appealed, and since his

trial precautions have been taken to limit media and spectator bias on the jury

(Constitutional Rights Foundation, 2000). One of the ways an accused can protect him or

herself from biased publicity is by asking the judge for a change of venue. However, this

is not often granted due to financial reasons (Constitutional Rights Foundation, 2000).

Some United States judges have instead tried to give an accused a fair trial, by restricting

22

the press from attending the trial. However, since this violates the First Amendment right of the American constitution, this may not be allowed (Constitutional Rights Foundation, 2000). This clearly illustrates that not only can pretrial publicity influence the jurors, but that the presence of the media at the trial in a spectator role, can have an impact as well.

1.4 Summary

After examining how jurors are selected, how they act and react during the trial and during deliberations, in some cases it may become apparent that the verdict the jury reaches has very little to do with the innocence or guilt of the accused. Many factors play a significant role in the jury's decision. Often the factors that play the most significant role in jury decision-making have very little, or nothing to do, with the accused's innocence or guilt. By applying social network analysis one can see very clearly the reasons for which jurors may not focus on the evidence to reach the verdict, but rely on other factors that are important to them in society. Most importantly, it is very idealistic to assume that jurors could separate all of their beliefs, attitudes, and social connections from the case, and view it with open minds. There will always be pressures, connections, and influences that play a significant role in the jury's verdict. Many studies in this area have not used social network analysis to examine jury decision-making. It would be beneficial to conduct a study that would use social network analysis to examine the strength of the connections that the jury creates in their network, as well as the influence of the primary and secondary circles on the jury's decision. These circles may have a significant impact on the jurors, which distracts them from the job at hand.

As it was described earlier in the paper, this social network is only constructed because of the accused. If the accused had not been charged with committing the crime, this network would not come to exist. Since this is the case, once the trial is over, the network dissolves, and each one of its members returns to their prior constructed networks. This is important to note, since most networks, once they are in place, go through changes or adaptation, but do not dissolve entirely (Breiger, Carley, & Pattison, 2002).

This newly formed network of jurors, lawyers, and spectators adapts many aspects of a social network for its duration. Similar to other networks, this network has sets of both formal and informal social roles. Formal roles can be defined as, "roles that are prescribed by groups, organizations or culture and are reflected in the designation of formal position" (Breiger et al., 2002, p. 121). In this network the judge occupies the formal position. The role of a judge comes with both written and unwritten norms and expectations. Even though there are many unwritten rules that the judge must follow, his/her role as a judge is a formal one, since that individual had to meet a specific set of qualifications to occupy the position (Tepperman & Curtis, 2004). The same is true for any formal role. In order to have obtained that role, an individual had to meet a set of expectations and they need to follow a set of written norms in order to maintain their position (Tepperman & Curtis, 2004). In order for the social dynamics of a network to function, there needs to be an interaction between the individuals who hold the formal and informal roles (Breiger et al., 2002). Among the informal roles, some individuals can have a more dominant role than other members of the group (Breiger et al., 2002). This means that in this network of the courtroom, the judge holds the very formal role, since she or he interacts with all group members, and keeps order and balance. Maintaining order and balance in a courtroom, is only one of many formal and written rules a judge needs to follow. However, within the circle there are individuals who hold informal but dominant roles, as well as formal roles.

Within the jury group, the foreman or forewoman occupies the formal role, since he or she is the leader of that group. Within the primary circle the lawyers would have formal roles, whereas other members of their teams occupy informal, but perhaps more or less dominate, roles. Media and the press, within the secondary circle, compose the formal position, while other spectators have informal roles. This is important, since it is the interaction between the individuals who hold the formal roles within the different groups of this network that are going to be vital for the verdict. How the individuals holding the different roles interact with one another will also show how cohesive the network is, since it will be the leaders of the different groups trying to influence one another, and especially the jury. The lawyers in the primary circle compete for leading roles, and making ties with the leader/leaders of the jury, and so do the leading members of the secondary circle. The ties made between the different leaders will represent a stance on the issue at hand, and the stronger the ties among the leaders, the more the verdict is impacted by that point of view (Breiger et al., 2002).

Many of the individuals who are leaders among the secondary circle have made prior connections with the members of the core circle before the trial. Different media and press reporters have delivered news or information to the members of the jury before the trial. As a result, their presence in the courtroom and the nature of their reaction to the evidence presented, may strongly impact the members of the jury.

The social influence network theory may clarify the intrapersonal/intragroup influences. This theory explains how inner influences that happen within groups affect a person's attitudes and opinions on issues and produce interpersonal agreements, including group consensus from an initial state of disagreement (Breiger et al., 2002, p. 89). The jury begins in a state of disagreement, and through the influences of others within the network they reach consensus. This integration of opinions or reaching of consensus is triggered by the representation of different opinions and the susceptibilities of group members to interpersonal influences. This is referred to as a social comparison trigger, where the pursuit to obtain correctness on an issue takes into account the current position of the group members on the issue. Group members' efforts to integrate opposing influences and to form socially validated positions on the issue at hand occur in a structural context that is a network of intrapersonal influences. This network has a profound impact on the opinion change process, as well as on the revised position that the group members may settle on. In order for opinion change to occur, factors such as efficiency in creating the content of an issue, as well as each member's contribution to establish the content and influence others in the group are important. This becomes clear in the following quote: "The content of persons equilibrium...on an issue, the efficiency with which this content is produced, and the relative net influence of each group member on others depends on the structure of the influence network in the group" (Breiger et al., 2002, p. 90). When the trial begins, there are many different opinions; however, the goal is to reach consensus and agreement by the time the trial is over, as represented by the verdict. The evidence presented during the course of the trial influences the changes to the jurors' opinions and creates agreement. Along with the evidence, there are other influences, such as the spectators whose goals are to change the jurors' opinions and induce them to agree with their point of view. All these influences take place in a formal context that is very structured and evolves according to many rules. It is the interpersonal influences that are going to form opinion change among the jury and lead to agreement. Much of this has not been applied to jury decision-making.

What may especially be important to study is the lawyers engagement or disengagement on the jurors verdict. The emotion of the lawyers is not evidence or relevant to the case at hand, however, it may play a grater role in the verdict than lawyer's education and professionalism. This in turn may mean that the accused obtains an unfair trial.

Since all individuals in the courtroom, have a role to play, and a script to follow studying the different roles and the unfolding script is key to having a better understanding of the current legal system in Canada, as well as, the changes that need to occur. In addition, lawyers are the central players in a case, thus, studying them first, may help researchers shine light on other aspects of legal procedures. Thus studying this by using social network analysis, may provide results that are more aligned with the real world phenomena, rather than, a laboratory experiment and having an understanding of the main players, will help with understanding the whole.

2   Methodology

The impact of the primary circle is especially beneficial to study. Those individuals who compose the primary circle are not only highly motivated to establish connections with the jurors, but it is their goal to do so. Their client's freedom depends upon the lawyers' performance, and thus depends heavily on the connection that the lawyers establish with the jury. Studying the connections that the two teams of lawyers form and their impact on the jury is very important.

More specifically, this study proposes to explore the following research questions and their implications. Does the lawyer's presentation of the case, especially his or her emotional connection with the jury, play a significant role in establishing connections with the members of the jury? If these connections are formed, they have an impact on the jurors, without the jurors interacting directly with the lawyers. If this is the case, it may be necessary to standardize lawyer behavior in order to mitigate any influence on the jury. As well, can a lawyer, by consciously trying to engage the jury in his/her presentation of the case, make a significant impact on the jury? The lawyer may be influencing the jury emotionally, rather than intellectually, thus the jury's decision may be based on feelings, rather than evidence. Conversely, can a lawyer negatively impact the members of the jury by consciously not connecting with the jury and rather than including them, exclude them completely?

In regard to the jurors, there are also questions that need to be answered regarding their interaction with the accused and the lawyers. Do the jurors use nonverbal communication to form connections with the lawyers? By being able to read the body language of the lawyer presenting the case, the jury will receive nonverbal information as to how the lawyer feels about the case and it will lead them to form an opinion about the case. Conversely, by reading the nonverbal communication of the jurors, the lawyers will understand how they feel about the case, and what methods of argument are effective. As well, this research will be looking at the leaders of cliques. Therefore it is a necessary piece of information to know if those jurors who are leaders in their everyday lives are the leaders in the deliberation room. Following from this point, the research will look at how the 12 individual jurors divide themselves into different cliques and sub-groups.

Does the type of connection between the two teams of lawyers and the leaders of the jury group play a role during deliberations? That is, if the leaders from the leading clique connect emotionally with a lawyer, they may have the power to influence the other members of the jury into conforming with their desired verdict.

There is the other side of the lawyers' emotional interaction: are the jurors influenced by the lawyer's emotional presentation, and adjust their opinions accordingly? It is theorized (Thagaard, 2004) that individuals look to each other to confirm their feelings. Thus, looking to other jurors and seeing the same emotion will confirm their feelings and opinions about the case. The above research questions will be answered by using an experimental research design.

2.1 Study Design

In the study four groups of 10-13 individuals each have been selected to represent the jury. Each group was assigned to one of four conditions:

1. Defense emotional disengagement of the jury versus prosecution neutral engagement.

2. Prosecution emotional disengagement versus defense neutral engagement.

3. Defense emotional engagement versus prosecution neutral engagement.

4. Prosecution emotional engagement versus defense neutral engagement).

That is, it was determined randomly which of these four experimental conditions in which each group would participate. It would have been preferable for participants to be randomly assigned to condition, but this was not possible because of scheduling restraints.

Once groups were randomly assigned to one of the four experimental conditions, they viewed a video of a mock murder trial, in which the lawyers either emotionally engaged the jury or did not. The same case was presented in the four conditions, however, one of the groups viewed a defense lawyer who was very disengaging, the other group saw a prosecution lawyer who was emotionally disengaging, and the last two groups viewed a defense lawyer who was very emotionally engaging and a prosecution lawyer who was emotionally engaged. The lawyer who was engaging maintained eye contact with the jurors and spoke directly to the jury, as well as leaned toward them, and acted in a manner that there was no doubt that the only audience he/she was talking to was the jury. The lawyer who was disengaged did not maintain eye contact, and simply delivered his argument in a non-emotional manner. He was not physically near the jury, and instead focused on his papers. In addition, each condition had a lawyer who was neutral. The individual who was neutral differs from the emotionally disengaged lawyer, by not trying to connect with, or in essence, excluding, the jury. This would mean that he delivered his information in a manner that showed the jury that he was neutral. Where the disengaged lawyer stood back and focused only on his paper, and did not maintain eye contact, a neutral lawyer, stood closer to the jury, but did not look directly at the jury. His glance once in awhile moved to the jury, but did not stay there too long, and did not focused on one particular person. This lawyer delivered the information precisely and with little emotion, but his body language was relaxed, as opposed to the disengaged lawyer, who was very tense, and the engaging lawyer who was very animated. Thus, this lawyer was professional, but did not consciously try to include or exclude the jurors.

The individuals chosen as the jury filled out a questionnaire (see Appendix B) before the trial began in order for the researcher to obtain demographic information about the jurors. The trial took three hours. After two segments of the trial jurors had a break during which they were able to interact with one another and their behavior was observed. Similarly, the researchers observed the jury's reaction to the lawyers' presentations during the trial. It was hypothesized that during the trial the jurors made both positive and negative connections with the two different teams of lawyers, which in turn impacted on their decision. A key role during deliberation depended on which jurors' clique made a positive/negative connection with which team of lawyers. If the leading clique made a positive connection with the defense or prosecution, that team of lawyers' presentation significantly influenced the verdict. Because of the stimuli were carefully controlled and the groups were randomly assigned to condition, the internal validity was relatively high, since the experimenters controlled for many of the threats to validity.

2.2 Participants

For the purpose of this study 43 participants were chosen. At first 48 were selected, however, do to their inability to take part in the entire study, only 43 remained. These individuals were assigned to groups based on their availability to come to the lab. Each group was then randomly assigned to condition. The 43 participants who represented the jury were recruited through advertisement in classrooms. The participants were undergraduate students in a variety of majors. Most of the participants were students in psychology 101. Amongst the 43 participants 18 were female while 24 were male and 1 participant did not provide information. There were 20 participants who identified themselves as Asian, 18 as Caucasian, 3 as brown, and 2 as other. The participants also were members of the major religions of the world. The sample thus contained both genders and people from a number of ethnic and religious backgrounds.

The participants that came from the Psychology 101subject pool. The participants were compensated for participating in this study by receiving three credits toward their Psychology 101 class. Most studies that have been conducted in this area used a university sample, not a community one. Since jurors who take part in a trial come from all walks of life, the combination of a university and a community sample would be more representative of the society at large, and therefore more generalizable (Warling & Peterson-Badali, 2003). However, due to lack of funding, it was not possible to use a community sample, as attrition is more likely to occur when participants are not adequately compensated.

A script of a murder trial was written (see Appendix A) and volunteers, as well as drama students from the University of Waterloo, were recruited to play the roles of the lawyers, the judge and the witnesses. The script included instructions for the actors who were playing the role of the lawyers as to the way they should act. For example, if they were to be the emotionally engaging lawyer, they were instructed to smile at the jury, speak directly to them, make eye contact with the jury, and lean toward the jury. If they were to be the emotionally disengaged lawyer, they were instructed to look straight ahead while delivering the lines, to not make eye contact with the jury, and to be very emotionally disengaged. The actors rehearsed the script, after which it was video recorded in the Kitchener Superior Court of Justice courtroom, and the jury viewed one of the four tapes. The same actors played the same roles in the different conditions, thus, all conditions of the jury were exposed to the same actors; the manipulation was the emotional engagement or emotional disengagement of the lawyers.

2.3   Problems in the Implementation of the Research Design

Since this study was run over three hours, there are several problems that arose. First, making sure that all of the individuals involved will be there for the entire study was an issue. That is, attrition is a common problem during lengthy studies. Second, giving up three hours of one's busy life in order to participate in a study, from which financial benefits were minimal, was a problem. The two coders recruited were Sociology students who had work experience in this area. The costs of the video production were minimal, as the actors and technical personnel were recruited on a volunteer basis from the Drama Department at the University of Waterloo and the audio-visual department.

2.4   Procedure

Once the jury participants were chosen and assigned to one of the four conditions, they were sequestered. During the time that the jurors were sequestered, they stayed in a room at St. Jerome's University where they were able to freely interact with one another, as well as watch the trial. However, the researchers were able to observe them through being in the same room with them, as well as having the coders and having a video-taped recording of their interactions. During this isolation their interactions were observed and their conversations were recorded at all times. This material was analyzed later to verify that cliques have been formed, and to subsequently validate the observations of the coders during the trial. The jurors observed the trial during which the lawyers reacted in accordance with the script and the condition. The eye contact serves as a point of connection between the jury and lawyers; therefore, without the eye contact, the connection between the jurors and the different teams did not form.

Partway through the trial (after the first few segments of the trial before the day's session is ended) the jurors had a break during which they were still sequestered, and observed again, by having their conversations videotaped and noted by coders. After this brief 10 minute break, everyone returned to watching the trial. Jurors had another 10 minute break during which they were able to interact freely with one another. The trial ended that day, and the jurors received judicial instructions, after which they deliberated. Before the deliberations started however, jurors gave their silent vote. The deliberations were recorded both by the coders and by video-taping. Once the jury delivered a verdict, they were free to go home. The instructions to the jurors stressed the point that they were not to discuss the case with other jurors or other people during the duration of the trial.

2.5 Measurement

As stated earlier, first when this new network is being formed only the accused links the jurors together. Thus, during the first experimental trial, when jurors are sequestered, the coders observed and noted the number, type and length of the contact that individual jurors have had with one another. Each juror was assigned a number from one to 12 and each time the observer saw a juror interacting with another he/she made a note of it. For example, when juror one introduced him/herself to Juror 5 and they talked for 4 minutes together, this interaction was recorded. In addition, nonverbal communication was noted as well. For example, smiles, leaning toward the other person, along with any physical contact, such as touching, were noted. Coders noted where the juror was sitting, the head of the table, or the sides, as well as the individual jurors' talkativeness. That is, how often did they speak, who did they address, and how long did they speak? How assertive were the jurors? Were they relaxed when they talked? That is, was their upper body relaxed when they talked? Did they speak without hesitation? Did they seem nervous or unsure? Was there a particular person that most jurors turn to and seem to listen to more than any other? Thus, in order to answer these questions, the coders were looking and coding the lengths, the types and the frequency of the interactions. In addition, they were looking for non-verbal interaction and coded these interactions in the same manner.

During the trial, the coders observed the jurors' nonverbal reaction to the lawyers and the evidence presented to them. Specifically, the jurors' nonverbal, as well as verbal reaction after the lawyer' presentation of the evidence was noted. The coders also looked for nonverbal communication between the jurors throughout the trial. All repetitive contact and communication signaled that a connection had been made and was being strengthened.

3   Results

In order to test the research questions laid out in the methodology section of the paper, it was first examined whether there were any significant differences between groups on characteristics such as, gender, race, religion, first language spoken, occupation, age or year in university. There were no significant differences between groups any of these variables (Mann-Whitney U's >36, p> .10). These finding suggest that there were no discernable difference between groups on these basic demographic variables.

To examine whether the differences between the lawyers engagement and disengagement while presenting their case to the jury influenced the jury's verdict a Kruskal-Wallis non-parametric was conducted. As shown in Table 1 there were no significant differences in voting between the groups before deliberation (Chi-Square with 3 d.f. = 2.47, p >.4), but after deliberation the effect of engaged lawyers seems to be evident. When the defense lawyer was engaged the jury came to a not-guilty verdict, but when the prosecution lawyer was engaged the jury came to a guilty verdict. The difference between conditions on the final vote was significant (Chi-Square with 3 d.f. = 25.06, p < .001).

Table 1

Voting Patterns by Time of Vote and Condition

Condition	Initial Vote	Final Vote
Defence Disengaged Prosecution Neutral	5 Guilty 5 Not Guilty	4 Guilty 6 Not Guilty
Prosecution Disengaged Defence Neutral	5 Guilty 4 Not Guilty 1 Undecided	8 Guilty 2 Not Guilty
Defence Engage Prosecution Neutral	7 Guilty 2 Not Guilty 1 Undecided	0 Guilty 12 Not Guilty
Prosecution Engaged Defence Neutral	9 Guilty 4 Not Guilty	13 Guilty 0 Not Guilty

Examining the data more closely there is no evidence that a disengaged lawyer had less influence than a neutral lawyer, but after deliberation an engaged lawyer appears to have more influence than a neutral lawyer. The effects should be interpreted with caution, however, because the final votes were not independent observations. Stronger conclusions could be made if each jury were treated as a unit of analysis—a project that would be much beyond the scope of this thesis.

The lawyer's engagement in the trial appears to have made a difference in the jurors' vote, but so did the role that individual jurors is likely to influence the verdict as well. As it was illustrated in the qualitative analysis, the jurors who showed leadership characteristics and took the role of the leader were significantly less likely to change their vote than those jurors who took the role of a follower. As it is shown in the diagrams and summaries of all conditions, those jurors who engaged others in conversations, initiated discussions, and took charge of the job at hand are seen not only to be well-connected with the other jurors, but also less likely to change their initial opinion. Those who are seen in the diagrams and the descriptions of the case as inactive, less engaged in discussions with others or taking charge of the situation are more likely to change their votes.

4   Analysis

4.1   Condition 1: Defence Disengaged, Prosecution Neutral

During the first part of the trial, only a few reactions occurred, but nothing that would be important, such as eye contact. Most jurors looked bored and gazed around the room (see Appendix C).

Break 1:

When the break begins, juror 7 asks general questions of the group, and does everything in his power to learn more about the others. Jurors 2 and 10 however, start many conversations, and take part in many as well. They are emerging as dominant figures and leaders of the group. All through the discussions jurors 2 and 10 have broken silences, started many conversations, and have contributed much to many discussions. In addition, jurors 7 and 8 are also very involved in conversations, but they have spent much time talking to the leaders 10 and 2. At the same time, jurors 3, 4, and 5 are very happy talking with each other. They join others, but they spend much time talking together. Similarly, jurors 6 and 9 are silent and do not contribute much to the discussions. During the next segment, jurors 4 and 5 were most active while watching the trial, but juror 4 mostly yawns and looked tired and bored.

Break 2:

During this break, jurors 7, 10 and 2 have been very active and have engaged others in general conversations. Jurors 2 and 10 continue to lead and have started many conversations; however, juror 7 has also been very active and has contributed much to many discussions. The major topic of conversation has been school; this seems to be the one topic that most jurors not only have in common, but are most comfortable talking about. During the next segment of the trial once again, jurors 4 and 5 were most active, laughing, yawning, and sleeping.

When the deliberations start, the first task at hand is to select a foreperson, and the groups unanimously chooses juror 2 who has been a foreperson before. During the discussion, the foreperson demonstrated leadership skills by engaging and challenging the jurors to discuss the trial and stay on topic. Most jurors took part in the conversation with the exception of juror 6 who was mostly silent. The first vote occurs and the results are as follows: 2, 4, 5, 6 and 9 vote guilty, while 3, 1, 7, 8, and 10 vote not guilty. The leaders are divided in their decision. In addition, juror 8 has taken an interest in the trial and is contributing much to supporting his group in presenting arguments and discussing the trial with others. The small sub-group of jurors 3, 4, and 5 has been broken and juror 3 has joined the opposite group from jurors 4 and 5. At the same time jurors, 1 and 6 have not contributed much, but are supporting the same vote.

After more discussions occur, another vote is conducted and it is juror 6 who changes his vote and votes not guilty. This is very interesting considering that this juror has not spoken or contributed to the group's discussions. It must be noted that the not guilty group has a leader and a very strong person, thus, it is two leaders arguing against only one leader. This may have been the key reason for which juror 6 has changed. Two strong voices, verses only one voice may have convinced this juror.

Final vote: juror 2, 4, 5, 9 guilty and 1, 3, 6, 7, 8, and 10 not guilty.

During the first moments of the trial jurors 4 and 5 were the most active jurors involved in the trial. Much of their behavior was not important, but they showed the most reaction. In addition, during the breaks, they spent much time talking with one another, and 4's wave to 5 may have suggested a prior acquaintance. These factors may have contributed to those two jurors supporting each other during deliberations. The most puzzling behavior is that of juror 6 who did not speak much during the trial, or after. All the other jurors have talked to each other and exchanged ideas and comments during the breaks. The verdict is surprising however, since during the trial the defense lawyer was very disengaged, while the crown was neutral.

Table 2

Direct Interactions among Jury Members: Condition 1

Direct interactions among jury members

Juror #	2	3	4	5	6	7	8	9	10	Degree	Summed	Strong tie
1	1	1	1		1	2		1	2	7	9	2
2						3	2		3	4	9	2
3			2	2					1	4	4	1
4				2						3	3	2
5										2	2	1
6						1		2	1	4	5	1
7							1		3	5	10	2
8									1	2	2	1
9									3	3	6	2
10										7	14	4

Degree = number of people with whom x interacts directly
Summed degree = number of recorded direct interactions
Strong tie degree = number of people with whom x interacts directly more than once

Large values are coloured

Figure 3

Social Network Diagram: Condition 1

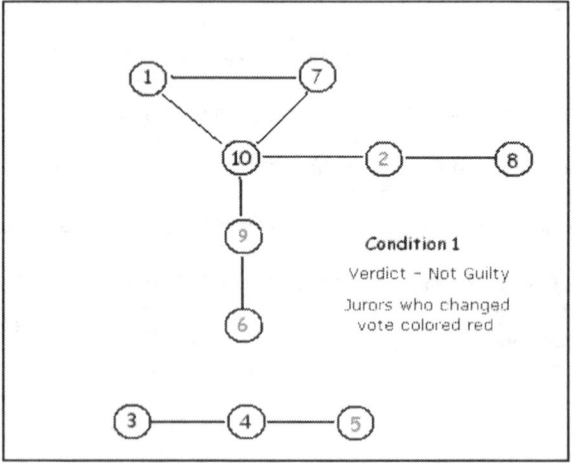

Condition 1
Verdict – Not Guilty
Jurors who changed
vote colored red

4.2   Condition 2: Prosecution Disengaged, Defence Neutral

First break:

During this first break (see Appendix D), juror 9 was a clear leader, starting conversations as well as contributing many ideas and thoughts to other people's conversations. Jurors 6, 4, 3, and 8 did not contribute much during this time. All the other jurors were engaged in many different conversations, and were doing their best to get to know one another. At the end of the first break it was only jurors 6 and 8 who were not engaged in conversations, and did not try to learn about others, or have others learn about them, especially juror 6.

During the second break, juror 9 continued to dominate and enjoyed many conversations with the other jurors. In addition, jurors 7, 2, and 5 were also very involved and engaged in conversations with others, along with juror 9. Juror 4 spoke when spoken to, and jurors 1 and 3 spoke here and there. At the same time jurors 6 and 8 were not involved at all, while juror 10 was mostly withdrawn from the discussions, but contributed more than jurors 6 and 8.

The deliberations begin, and juror 4 becomes the foreperson. This juror is the foreperson, but only because he is in Legal studies and Criminology, and has knowledge of the Canadian legal system. The first vote occurs and the results are as follows: jurors 8, 9, and 2 first degree murder, jurors 1 and 3 second degree, and 10, 7, 6, and 5, not guilty while juror 4 is undecided.

When the discussions begin again and continue, the two guilty groups join together and support each other, while juror 6 continues to be withdrawn and not contribute to the discussion. Juror 9 continues to be the leader and argues with the other

41

jurors. The guilty group works together, and stands united against the not guilty group. Thus, after the second vote the results are as following, jurors 1, 2, 3, 4, 8, and 9 vote guilty of second-degree murder while jurors 5, 6, 7, and 10 vote not guilty.

After this second vote juror 4 has made up his mind, while all other jurors have stayed with their votes. The guilty group continues to work together and argue for a guilty verdict, while juror 5 is single-handedly fighting the not guilty battle. It is becoming clear that even though juror 4 is the foreperson, juror 9 is the most dominate one, and is the leader for the guilty group, while juror 5 is the leader for the not guilty group and is single-handedly battling with the others. Thus, jurors 9 and 5 are the leaders.

The final vote takes place and it is 8 guilty to 2 not guilty. Jurors 1, 2, 3, 4, 6, 8, 9, and 10 vote guilty. Jurors 5 and 7 vote not guilty. Jurors 6 and 10 changed, but these two were the least involved jurors, especially juror 6. Juror 7 was wavering, but in the end did not change his mind.

Table 3

Direct Interactions among Jury Members: Condition 2

Direct interactions among jury members

Juror #	2	3	4	5	6	7	8	9	10	Degree	Summed degree	Strong tie degree
1	5	6	1	4	0	2	6	13	1	8	38	4
2		1	1	4	0	12	1	10	2	9	36	3
3			4	2	0	1	1	5	0	7	20	2
4				2	0	0	0	2	0	5	10	0
5					0	2	2	9	3	8	28	1
6						0	0	0	0	0	0	0
7							1	6	0	6	24	2
8								3	1	7	15	1
9									0	7	48	5
10										4	7	0

Degree = number of people with whom x interacts directly
Summed degree = number of recorded direct interactions
Strong tie degree = number of people with whom x interacts directly more than 4 times

Large values are coloured

42

Figure 4

Social Network Diagram: Condition 2

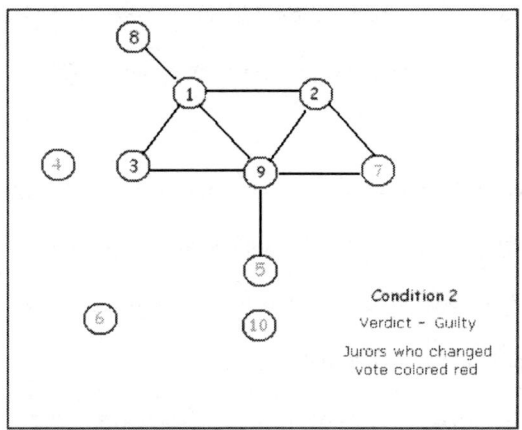

Condition 2
Verdict - Guilty
Jurors who changed
vote colored red

4.3   Condition 3: Defense Engaged, Prosecution Neutral

As the trial begins, all jurors are paying close attention to the trial (see Appendix E). Juror 2 takes notes all through the first segment of the trial, while the others watch and listen. The first break begins.

During the first break, the jurors have divided themselves into pairs, and mostly talked with only one other person. There are very few group discussions. Thus, after this first break, most of the conversations were about school, programs of study and professors. The conversations were mostly within small groups, or pairs, but juror 8 was the most animated and showed leadership by engaging others in conversations. Juror 8 had most of his conversations with juror 9 and they seemed the most close together. At the same time, jurors 1 and 2 were the most uninterested and unengaged.

As the second segment of the trial begins, most jurors are listening intently. Juror 2 continues to take notes through this part of the trial. Jurors 9 and 8 are the most active, laughing, smiling, and exchanging looks. Juror 9 joins juror 2 in taking notes, and part way through this second segment it is both juror 2 and 9 who are taking notes. The second break is announced.

During this second break, jurors 9 and 8 continued to talk together, and engaged others in conversations. Jurors 1 and 2 spoke the least. The others talked and were engaged in conversations all around, but no one spoke as much as jurors 8 and 9. The break is over and all jurors turn their attention to the trial.

During this last segment of the trial, juror 9 and 2 took the most notes. Other jurors were listening to the trial, but it was juror 9 and 2 who took notes, and it was juror 9 who had the most reactions to the testimony.

The deliberations begin, and they start with an open vote. Their first open vote results are as follows: jurors 1, 3, 5, 6, 7, and 8, 9 vote guilty, while jurors 2 and 8 were voting not guilty. Juror 4 was not sure, and did not decide on his vote at this time.

Once the open vote is over, juror 9 speaks up about selecting a foreperson, and the group suggests that he take the position. He does, and this time it is because he was the only one who spoke up about it, and not because he was studying Legal Studies and Criminology or had jury experience, like in the previous two conditions.

After the first vote, it is 7 jurors who vote guilty, 2 not guilty and 1 has not decided. Before the second vote takes place, it is juror 2 arguing for a not guilty verdict, and juror 7 is most engaged in the discussions that take place. During these talks, juror 7 changes his mind, and starts supporting juror 2 in the not guilty verdict. Other jurors are swaying.

The second vote occurs and is as following: voting for guilty of second-degree murder are jurors 1, 3, 4, and 8. Voting not guilty are jurors 2, 5, 6, 7, 9, and 10. Thus, after the second vote, the not guilty group is dominating, even though after the first one, it was the guilty group who had more supporters.

During this last segment of deliberations, it was jurors 7, 8, 9, 10 and 2 who continued arguing their points, and jurors 4, 5, and 6 mostly listened and only occasionally offered a comment. In the end, all jurors were united in their not guilty verdict.

During the deliberations, even though juror 9 was the foreperson, it was juror 2 who spoke up the most and made most arguments. He was the juror who stood by his decision and convinced others that the not guilty verdict is the only verdict that should occur in this case. Juror 2 started in the minority, since only juror 10 was in agreement with him; however, after the deliberations were over, the other 7 jurors changed their vote. Juror 10 supported juror 2, but juror 2 was unquestioningly the most dominating voice. Jurors 3, 4, and 5 spoke up the least, as did juror 6. Only here and there, did these jurors make a comment; they did not take a leading role in most of the discussions. It was mostly jurors 2, 8, 9, 10, and 7 who argued and discussed the case. Juror 1 was totally silent and was not heard at all. Thus, jurors 8 and 9 who spoke much during the trial, and juror 2 who was taking notes, were the key players during the deliberations.

Table 4

Direct Interactions among Jury Members: Condition 3

Direct interactions among jury members

Juror #	2	3	4	5	6	7	8	9	10	Degree	Summed degree	Strong tie degree
1	4	1	1	1	0	0	1	1	2	7	11	0
2		2	1	1	0	9	7	9	7	8	40	4
3			1	1	1	3	5	5	3	9	22	2
4				3	0	0	2	1	0	6	9	0
5					0	2	3	1	0	4	12	0
6						3	1	0	4	4	9	0
7							9	4	9	7	39	3
8								14	5	9	47	5
9									7	8	42	4
10										7	37	4

Degree = number of people with whom x interacts directly
Summed degree = number of recorded direct interactions
Strong tie degree = number of people with whom x interacts directly more than 4 times

Large values are coloured

Figure 5

Social Network Diagram: Condition 3

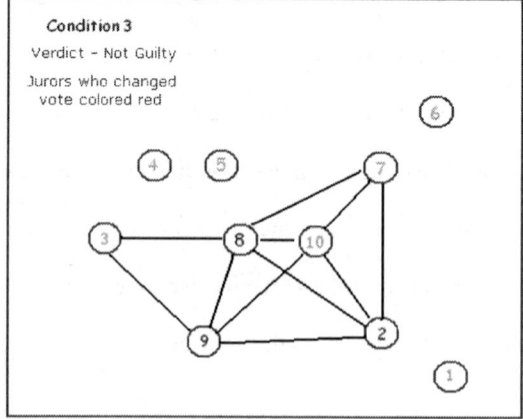

Condition 3
Verdict - Not Guilty
Jurors who changed vote colored red

4.4   Condition 4: Prosecution Engaged, Defense Neutral

During the first segment of the trial, a few jurors looked tired, but overall, all watched and paid attention to the trial (see Appendix F). The first break arrives, and the jurors are ready for it.

During this break, it was juror 3 who started many conversations with a variety of other jurors. This juror was most active and was trying to get to know others. At the same time, jurors 7, 2, 6, and 1 were fairly quiet, especially juror 7. This group of jurors enjoyed many small conversations within pairs, rather than having small group discussions or large group talks. The same pairs talked through the break, and only a few jurors tried to engage others in conversations.

The break is over and jurors turn their attention back to the trial. During this segment of the trial, mostly juror 1 was active by taking notes as well as doodling, and juror 7 looked tired all through the segment. The other jurors listened to the trial, and mostly shifted in their seats and looked around the room, but showed no other signs of activity. The second break is announced, and the jurors start talking.

During this break, the same people talked together as during the previous break. Juror 7 also continued to look tired, and juror 2 did not speak much. Most of the jurors did not engage those across the table from them in conversations; they only talked to those next to them. There were many intense conversations, especially between jurors 11, 4, and 8. Even though they did not talk together, there were no uncomfortable silences, and jurors were working on getting to know one another. The trial was ready to start again.

In this last segment of the trial, juror 1 continued to take notes, while juror 7 continued to look tired. The trial is now over, and the jurors turn their attention to the deliberations. Juror 4 becomes the foreperson, since no one else wanted the job. Different from the other groups, no open vote occurs at the beginning of the deliberations, but instead jurors jump right into discussing the trial. Juror 4 leads the group, and is very organized in his role as foreperson.

All through the first part of the deliberations, all jurors were involved in the discussion, bring up points, and discuss different angles of the crime. Juror 12, however, was the only one arguing for a not guilty verdict, all other jurors are arguing for guilty. The discussions continue. Juror 4 continues to be the leader, and since he believes that the accused is guilty, he is very strong in presenting his evidence for a guilty verdict. All jurors are involved in discussions, and there are several who believe that the accused is not guilty.

Juror 4 asks the group for a vote, in which jurors 9, 10, 11, and 12 vote not guilty, while jurors 1, 2, 3, 4, 5, 6, 7, 8, and 13 vote guilty. This is a key point, since juror 13 is voting for guilty, however, in the end he will be the only one holding out and wishing to vote not guilty. As the discussion starts again, jurors 9, 10, 11, and 12 argue for a not guilty verdict. After a few minutes of discussions, during which they were attacked by the guilty group, juror 10 changes his mind and is now full-heartedly arguing for a guilty verdict. Jurors 9, 11, and 12 have also changed their votes. Juror 13 was the only one who said not guilty, but after juror 4 and the others, started arguing with him, juror 13 changed his mind. There was much pressure on this juror to change his mind from the whole group, who wanted to go home and juror 13 was the only one holding them back.

Table 5

Direct Interactions among Jury Members: Condition 4

Direct interactions among jury members

Juror #	2	3	4	5	6	7	8	9	10	11	12	13	Degree	Summed degree	Strong tie degree
1	0	0	2	7	1	0	1	2	5	0	5	1	8	24	3
2		4	1	0	1	2	0	0	1	2	1	1	8	13	0
3			7	0	3	10	3	3	3	2	3	1	10	39	2
4				3	5	2	5	5	10	9	9	2	12	60	7
5					2	1	1	1	4	1	2	2	10	24	1
6						4	0	1	12	4	9	1	11	43	3
7							0	0	4	1	4	1	9	29	1
8								4	1	4	0	0	7	19	1
9									3	0	3	6	9	28	2
10										4	14	4	12	65	4
11											3	1	10	31	1
12												1	11	54	4
13				?									11	21	1

Degree = number of people with whom x interacts directly
Summed degree = number of recorded direct interactions
Strong tie degree = number of people with whom x interacts directly more than 4 times

Large values are coloured

Figure 6

Social Network Diagram: Condition 4

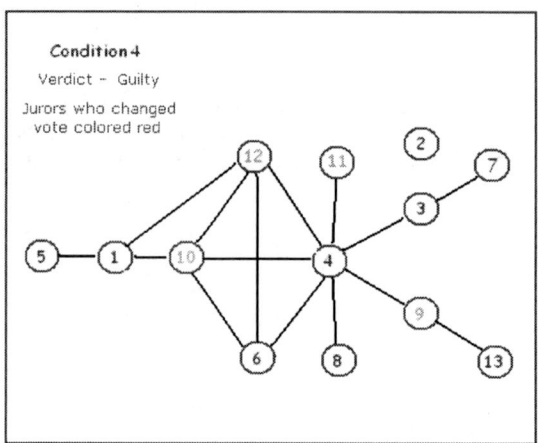

5   Discussion

This paper took the research of jury decision-making a step further, and examined the influence of lawyers on the jurors' decision, while the lawyers try to establish invisible connections with jurors. Other researchers have focused on emotional interaction between lawyers and jurors; however, in this study researchers examined the impact of the lawyers' emotional engagement, and disengagement on the jurors' verdict. In addition, research focused on analyzing the patterns of interactions between the jurors themselves while they watched the trial and deliberated on the verdict. Social network analysis was not used in this type of research before, and even though this study was unable to conduct a full social network analysis due to the limitation of the data, very rudimentary network analysis has been conducted.

Two types of analyses have been conducted, all answering the research questions, and all analyses were significant. The first level of analysis was quantitative, shedding light on the pattern of vote change between the different groups, as well as supporting the qualitative analysis. This analysis also looked within each group to determine the patterns of voting. This last level of analysis focused on describing jurors' behaviour, interactions, and the unfolding interactions between jurors as they sought to reach a verdict.

Since all groups saw the same trial and the only variation between the four different conditions was the lawyer's emotional engagement, it was important to look at whether the groups were equally and randomly distributed. There were no significant differences between groups on a number of demographic variables, thus, the groups seemed to be roughly equivalent.

In examining the voting patterns of the juries there was some evidence that the effect of the lawyers' level of engagement impacted jurors' votes. As it was predicted, when the defense lawyer was engaged and strongly believed in her client's innocence, she was able to convince the jurors that the accused was not guilty of the crime; at least this was the verdict after deliberation of the jury. Similarly, when the Crown attorney believed that the accused was guilty of the crime, even though she presented the same evidence to the jurors as in the other conditions, the jurors believed her patterns of events, and voted accordingly, but again only reaching a unanimous verdict after deliberation.. Therefore, the lawyers' engagement, enthusiasm, and strong belief her arguments seems to have a significant impact on the jury's verdict. In addition, the results suggest that jurors are equally affected when a lawyer is engaged or disengaged. During the disengaged trial jurors listen, but do not take the lawyer's performance into consideration when making their decision. A defense lawyer who is disengaged has a choice in the case that he/she is representing, whereas, a crown lawyer does not. Thus, it can be speculated that while the crown attorney simply does his/her job, defense who is engaged strongly believes in the client.

This suggests that jurors make decisions based on their emotional involvement in the trial, and not the evidence. The evidence in each experimental condition was exactly the same, and the only difference was the delivery of that evidence to the jurors. Even though this was a very short and simple case with very few experts and very uncomplicated testimonies, the voting patterns were predicted based on how the lawyers delivered their case to the jury and not on the content of the evidence. This strongly suggests that work needs to be conducted to standardize the delivery of evidence by each lawyer, since otherwise, the decisions will be made based on emotion and not on evidence.

The second level of analysis focused on each condition in turn, and included an examination of the jurors' interactions with each other throughout the trial and the deliberations. The results of this part of the study show the beginnings of social networks, as well as developing patterns within sub-groups of each larger group. The first condition of the study presented jurors with a defense lawyer who was very disengaged, while the prosecution lawyer was neutral. All through the lawyers' presentations jurors witnessed the defense lawyer's lack of enthusiasm for her work, as well as disinterest, and boredom. This lawyer did not fight for her client. Quite the opposite, she went through the motions, and lacked passion. The prosecution did not show much emotion, either for or against the client, but she was very professional and did her work well. It was hypothesized that in this condition the verdict would favor the prosecution, since the defense lawyer did not inspire the jurors with the confidence and conviction that her client was not guilty of the crime. This however, was not the case, and the verdict came back favoring the defense, but not all jurors believed in this verdict. The split in the verdict was 6 jurors who voted not guilty, while 4 jurors voted guilty during the final vote.

Looking at jurors interactions during the trial and deliberations will give insight into this unexpected verdict. All participants in this condition were students, and this was a connection that they used to get to know one another. Many conversations were about school, professors, tests, and courses that each juror has taken or is intending to take. Very early however, it became apparent who was the leader. In this condition two jurors emerged as strong leaders, who guided the others in conversations, and were very comfortable asking others questions, and guiding the group during breaks. Similarly, cliques were hinted at during the interactions between jurors while they were on break from the trial. Jurors 3, 4, and 5 enjoyed talking together, and were observed to have conversations together at different points during the trial. Following from this, jurors 7 and 8 enjoyed talking to the leaders and spent much time in conversation with these two individuals. There were two jurors, however, who did not take part in conversations, and who looked very uninvolved in the happenings around them. Thus, when the trial came to an end and the jurors were ready to elect a foreperson, one of the group leaders became the foreperson. This person was not only already established as a leader of this group, but also had past experience as a juror. This pattern of behavior has been observed and found by other researchers in other trials. Thus, this finding supports Hans & Vidmar's (1986) findings, which showed that previously established leaders become the forepersons, as well as those who have experience in these matters. This was the case in this study as well. Choosing a foreperson, took very little time, and the person who was chosen, was a group leader and had experience in this matter.

In this condition there were two leaders, and after the first open vote, they were in opposition. The foreperson and one of the leaders were in opposition with juror 10, who also showed much leadership during the trial, and with whom the foreperson was engaged in many conversations with jurors 7 and 8. After the first vote, juror 10 was in agreement with both of those jurors, with whom he spent much time talking and interacting. The foreperson, however, was alone, and even though he agreed with the others on many topics that they talked about, they had a difference of opinions when it came to the verdict. Thus, as the deliberations occurred, few changes took place, one of which was that the leaders were not in agreement, and the small sub-group of 3, 4, and 5 was divided. Juror 3 believed that the accused was not guilty, while jurors 4 and 5 believed that the accused was guilty of the crime. Thus, juror 10 was supported by other jurors with whom he interacted with much before, and juror 8 had taken much interest in the trial. Juror 8 argued points along with juror 10, against the foreperson. The not guilty group had two strong voices, as well as another juror who made a connection with them. On the other hand, the foreperson, even though he had very good leadership skills and guided the discussions well, was the only strong voice in the guilty group.

When another vote took place, the juror who had the least to say during the entire trial was the one who made the difference in the verdict. This juror changed his mind, and without explanations, moved to the not guilty group. It could be deduced that the strength of two voices, persuaded this juror that the not guilty verdict was the right one. This group was stronger and supported each other much more than the guilty group. Thus, even though this was not the prediction, this verdict followed a pattern found by other researchers. Hans & Vidmar (1986) found alliances and supports of jurors regarding each other's point were important during deliberations. This was the case in this current study. Similarly, once a point of view was presented to the group and supported by others who were aligned with the leaders, the information grew in power, and others took note of it and followed the lead (Hans & Vidmar, 1986). Thus, the views of leaders and the support that the leader obtains from other jurors is key in reaching many verdicts, more so than lawyer's presentation of the case. Thus, it is not the evidence that matters, but the opinions of the leaders of the groups.

The second condition of the study involved a defense lawyer who presented her case to the jurors in a neutral manner, while the prosecution was unengaged, and uninterested in the matter at hand. In this condition, similar to the first condition and previously established patterns, the foreperson of this group had experience in the area of legal studies and was voted to be the leader of the group. This individual was not the leader who emerged from discussions during breaks and the trial; however, the group felt that since he had experience and knowledge in this area he should be the one who would best guide them in the discussion (Hans & Vidmar, 1986). Juror 9, however, was the clear leader from the very beginning of the trial, and during the deliberations, even though he was not the foreperson, he proved to be equally powerful and guided conversations, challenged jurors, and was able to sway other jurors to support him in his opinion and verdict. At the same time, juror 5 was single-handedly fighting the battle for a not guilty verdict. This juror had very few supporters, and those who supported him, did not join in or add support to his points. The guilty group, all through the discussions, followed their leader, and supported one another's points, ideas, and arguments. Thus, this group had very powerful arguments and was much stronger as a team; therefore, it should not be surprising that the final vote was eight guilty to two not guilty. Furthermore, the foreperson supported the leader, and they stood united in the guilty verdict. Thus, once again, the negative presentation of the case by the prosecution did not make a difference in the case, but strong leadership was able to guide the group to support their opinion. In these first two conditions, the verdicts did not go in the same direction as the hypothesis, and it may be due to the fact that the behavior of the unengaged lawyers was so unexpected, that it drew the jurors' attention, as opposed to alienating the jury. More studies need to be conducted to fully understand the reason for why jurors in these two cases voted differently than predicted.

In the third condition, in which the defense was engaged whereas the prosecution was neutral, jurors voted as predicted. This third group of jurors followed a slightly different pattern of behavior from the other two groups. In the end, however, they were united in their decision. In this group of jurors, one juror in particular took notes throughout the trial, and even though this juror was uninvolved in conversations during breaks with other jurors, during deliberation this juror became very active. Another juror joined him in taking notes, but this was not until the last segment of the trial. There were two jurors--jurors 8 and 9--who were the most active jurors during breaks. Juror 9 was also the one who took notes towards the end of the trial. These two jurors spoke together and with others. What was different in this group was that the jurors spoke mostly in pairs, and very few small group discussions occurred. The same jurors spoke together, from break to break, and only on occasion did they speak with others in the group.

Similar, to previous research, and what was observed in the other two conditions, the foreperson was selected very quickly. This time however, the foreperson spoke first during deliberations, and thus was chosen for the job. It was juror 9, who was very active during the breaks, and already established as one of the leaders. Thus, similar to Hans and Vidmar's (1986) findings, the juror who spoke first during deliberations was the foreperson in this case. When the deliberations started, only two jurors, 2 and 10, voted not guilty, while 7 jurors voted guilty, and 1 juror was undecided. This is very interesting, since at the beginning of the deliberations the majority was voting guilty. In the end however, they were all united in a not guilty verdict.

As the deliberations took place, juror 2, who took the most notes throughout the trial, was very active in presenting his arguments. This juror was not only very active, but presented powerful arguments, that almost single-handedly persuaded the others to vote not guilty. Shortly after this juror started presenting his arguments, some of the other jurors from the guilty group changed their minds and joined juror 2 in his fight for a not guilty verdict. Juror 9, who was the foreperson, after the second vote, is one of the jurors who joined juror 2 in the argument for a not guilty verdict. Thus, it was one juror who was not even engaged during the breaks in discussions with other jurors, and did not establish connections with others, that was the one with the strongest influence. This juror was not persuaded from his convictions from the beginning of the deliberations, but instead took on the role of the leader and presented his arguments in such a way that the others were convinced. This juror also obtained the support of the leaders, who during the second vote were already supporting him in his quest for a not guilty verdict. The verdict of this grouped supported the hypothesis. The defense lawyer, who was very engaged, was able to persuade two people that his account of the events was a true one, and the one juror who supported this lawyer was able to convince the others that this was the case. Thus, the connections that the lawyers make with jurors, even if it is only one or two jurors, may play a significant role in the final verdict.

In the last condition of the study, in which the prosecution was engaged and the defense was neutral, the final verdict was as predicted by the hypothesis. This time however, the majority of the jurors believed that the accused was guilty and argued accordingly. In this condition, similar to the third condition, jurors enjoyed conversations in very small groups of two and three, and did not speak with those jurors who were not sitting close to them. They all spent much time getting to know one another, with the exception of juror 7 who looked tired and was withdrawn from conversations during the breaks. Similar to the third condition, the foreperson was the juror who spoke first and volunteered for the position. This juror was very active during small group discussions, especially with jurors 11 and 8. In addition, juror 1 took notes during the trial, similar to juror 2 from condition three.

The foreperson in this condition took the role of the leader very seriously and was very active in directing the group, organizing information, and persuading others. This juror, along with a few others, believed the accused to be guilty from the start and did not waver in his beliefs, but instead convinced, or pressured others to support him in the guilty verdict. Once again, the leader and the foreperson of this group had a lot of power, and used his power to persuade others that their point of view was correct (Hans &

58

Vidmar, 1986). Furthermore, this group of jurors, similar to other groups, had a goal: to arrive at a verdict as soon as possible and return to their daily lives (Scott, 2000). They were highly motivated to get the job done and conducted the deliberation in the most efficient manner. Thus, the group did not go through many links to achieve this goal, but took the most direct route (Scott 2000). This group of jurors, however, did their job differently from others: they did not have an open vote, but instead jumped straight into discussing the evidence.

When the vote did occur, 9 jurors voted guilty, while only 4 jurors voted not guilty. Only one juror however, actively argued for a not guilty verdict, and that juror in the end was pressured to change his mind and did so. Juror 13 is the most interesting one, since he voted guilty; however in the end, he was the only juror who wanted the verdict to be not guilty. When juror 12 changed his mind, juror 13 took up his spot and argued for a not guilty verdict.

The not guilty supporters in this condition were under much pressure from the leaders and the others to change their minds. All four jurors who at first voted not guilty changed their votes, and juror 13 who started by voting guilty and then changed to not guilty held out the longest. In the end, this juror gave in to the pressure, and the verdict was guilty. In this condition, one can see clearly the impact of the Crown attorney on the jurors. The majority of them believed that the accused was guilty, and were convinced not only by the evidence presented to them by this lawyer, but also by the manner that the material was presented to them. Thus, the lawyer's presentation of the case to the jurors appears to play a significant role during deliberations.

The findings of this study also show that those who describe themselves as leaders and take part in team activities are less likely to change their votes. This is similar to what Hans & Vidmar (1986) found. They found that those who have a higher education, occupy a high status in society and are well-connected are viewed as experts in the jury room during deliberations. Since others see these individuals as leaders and experts, it should not be surprising that the leaders are less likely to change their votes. The leaders convince others that their ideas and opinions are right, and thus, they do not believe they are wrong. As a result, they do not change their minds, but stick with their ideas, and are not persuaded by others. Those who do not have this kind of experience start questioning their opinions and ideas, and change their votes to be in agreement with the leaders. The leaders may not have the best recollection of the trial, but they are confident about their recollection, which is the key. Other jurors may not be confident about their memories, even though their recollection may be much better than the leaders. Thus, the verdict will be based on the leaders' recollection, and this may be the reason why the leader will be less likely to change their vote (Prichard & Keenan, 2002). Thus, the model which was the first level of this study's analysis shed light on the factors that may have been important in the jurors changing their verdicts or not.

The data from this research showed that the lawyers' presentation of the case, especially his/her emotional connection with the jury, does play a significant role in establishing invisible connections with the jurors. It was observed that connections between jurors and lawyers were made, without personal contact with the lawyers. In this case especially, the jurors saw a video; therefore, they were unable to personally meet or talk with the lawyers. Much more research needs to be conducted; however, standardizing lawyers' presentation of the case to the jurors may help in reducing emotional influence of lawyers of the jurors.

In addition, the lawyer's conscious attempt to engage the jurors in her presentation of the case had a significant impact on the jurors. Thus, the lawyer may be influencing jurors emotionally, rather than intellectually. Furthermore, those presentations of the case by the lawyers, in which they consciously tried to exclude jurors from the testimony proved to bring the opposite results. The jurors formed invisible connections with lawyers; however, little non-verbal communications between jurors and lawyers was observed. This may be due to the trial being presented to the jurors in a video format, where it was much harder for the jurors to communicate nonverbally with the lawyers. The lawyers were unable to read the jurors' nonverbal messages. Thus, it may be beneficial to conduct this study in a manner in which the lawyers deliver the case in person to the jurors.

It was found that the connections that the leaders of the jury make with the different teams of lawyers do have an impact on the final verdict. It was seen that those leaders who were emotionally influenced by the teams of lawyers presenting the case were able to persuade others, even if they were in the minority at the start of the deliberations. Similar to what the Social Influence Network theory has described, the jurors started in a state of disagreement, however, the inner influences of jurors led to not only attitude change of many of the jurors, but also produced agreement on the issue (Brieger et al., 2002). The jurors started in a state of disagreement, but through discussing the trial with others they reached a state of agreement.

61

Many jurors in this study were pressured to deliver a verdict by their peers in the jury room. Unlike a real trial, these groups of jurors were not pressured by their social networks to deliver a verdict that was desired by their social groups. This was a mock trial that was not publicized; thus, jurors in this case were pressured only by those who wanted to finish their work quickly and return to other personal activities. This may not be the case in regular jury trials. Since this was an experimental setting, this was one of the limitations of the trial (Scott, 2000; Kassin & Wrightsman, 1988).

In addition to this limitation of this study, there are several more. First, the sample consisted of university students, and although this created a bond between them and was a connection that many of them used to learn more about one another, this would not be the case in a jury trial. Thus, it may be beneficial to use a community sample while conducting this kind of study in the future. Also, a larger sample would allow for stronger statistical results. Thus, a much larger sample would be recommended for future research. This was not possible in this study, due to financial constraints. Similarly, the trial in itself was much shorter than a typical murder trial would have been. Being able to prepare a much longer trial, with more complex themes and testimony may result in jurors looking to lawyers' non-verbal cues since they would be unable to follow the technical aspects of the trial. This was not the case in this trial, and all jurors were able to follow the development of the trial with ease. The jurors had only three hours to view the trial, learn more about each other, and then discuss the trial. This time was too short to attempt to build strong connections among the jurors. The jurors were establishing connections, and the beginnings of cliques were observed, however, these relationships did not have a chance to develop. Thus, a trial that would have lasted two days, where the jurors had time to spend with one another would be beneficial. Threats to external validity were not a problem in this study, since even though participants were involved in a laboratory experiment, they very quickly adapted to the experiment and reacted to the mock trial as if it were a real trial.

These are only some limitations of this study and suggestions for improvements in the future. Following from this research it would be beneficial, to not only replicate this study with a much larger sample, and a more complex trial that lasts much longer, but the study of the impact of spectators on jurors decision may be beneficial.

This research has shown that the lawyers' emotional presentation of a case does play a significant role during the deliberations, as well as that the impact on the leader of a group may have a large impact on the verdict. Thus, by standardizing the lawyers' presentation of the case by restricting their movement in the courtroom, as well as advising the lawyers to maintain eye contact with the jurybut not to engage in other interactions with the jurors, may improve our judicial system and yield better results.

References

Bottoms B. L., Nysse-Carris K. L., Harris T., & Tyda K. (2003). Jurors' Perceptions Of Adolescent Sexual Assault Victims Who Have Intellectual Disabilities. *Law and Human Behavior, 27* (2), 205-223.

Breiger, R., Carley, K., & Pattison, F. (Eds.). (2002). *Dynamic Social Network Modeling and Analyses: Social Influence Network Theory.* Washington D.C.: National Academies Press.

Bull Kovera M. & Russano M. B.& McAuliff B. (2002). Assessment of the Commonsense Psychology Underlying Daubert; Legal Decision Makers' Abilities to Evaluate Expert Evidence in Hostial Work Environment Case. *Psychology Public Policy and Law, 8*(2), 180-198.

Constitutional Rights Foundation. Bill of Rights in Action. (2000). *The Right To An Impartial Jury Trial and a Free Press.* Retrieved March 22, 2004, from www.interscience.wiley.com.

Erikson, B. (1988). In *Social Structure: A Network Approach.* Wellman, B. & Berkowitz, S.D. (Eds.). New York: Cambridge University Press; p.99-121.

Hans, V. P., & Vidmar, Neil. (1986). *Judging the Jury Publisher.* New York, New York: Plenum Press.

Hobbs, P. (2003) "Is That What We Are Here About?" A Lawyer's Use of Impression Management in a Closing Argument at Trial. *Discourse and Society,14*(3), 273-290.

Kassi, S. M., & Wrightsman, L. S. (1988). *The American Jury on Trial.* New York, New York: Hemisphere Publishing Corporation.

Marsden, P. (1994). In *Advances in Social Network Analysis: Research in Social and Behavioral Sciences.* Wasserman, S. & Galaskiewicz, J. (Eds.). California: Sage Publications; p.1-22.

Pritchard M. E., & Kennan J. M., (2002). Does Jury Deliberation Really Improve Jurors Memories? *Applied Cognitive Psychology, 16,* 589-601.

Scott J. (2000). *Social Network Analysis: A Handbook* (2nd ed.). London: Sage Publications.

Tepperman, Lorne & Curtis, James (2004). *Sociology: A Canadian Perspective.* Ontario: Oxford University Press.

Thagard, Paul. (unpublished). Emotional Consensus in Group Decision Making.

Thagard, Paul. (2003). "Why wasn't OJ convicted? Emotional coherence in legal inference." *Cognition & Emotion, 17*(3), 361-383.

Warling, Diane & Peterson-Badali, Michele. (2003).The Verdict on Jury Trials for Juveniles: The Effects of Defendant's Age on Trial Outcomes. *Journal of Behavioral Science and the Law, 21,* 63-82.

Worthington D. L., Stallard M., Price J. M., & Goss P. J., (2002). Hindsight Bias, Daubert, and the Silicone Breast Implant Litigation: Making the Case for Court-appointed Experts in Complex Medical and Scientific Litigations Journal; Psychology, Public Policy and Law, 8 (2), 154-179.

Appendix A – Trial Script

Characters

Sabrina Gray "accused"

Steven Klein "victim"

Mark Tyler "victim's roommate"

Jim Thomson "police Officer, first on the scene"

Paul King "defense Lawyer"

Kim Wild, roommate, "witness"

John Steel "judge"

Amanda Moss, "bartender"

The Charge

Sabrina Gray, a 22 year old University of Waterloo student is accused of murdering her boyfriend Steven Klein, a 23 year old WLU student.

The Evening Before the Murder.

Sabrina and Steven had an argument in Sabrina's apartment where she accused Steven of cheating on her with another girl that they both knew. Steven denied the accusation and claimed that they were studying for a test together. This seemed to make Sabrina even more upset, and she kept repeating she hated him, that he was a lying snake, that she wished that she had never met him and hoped he would die because of the pain he had caused her. This argument took place at about 9 P.M. and was overheard by Sabrina's roommate Kim Wild. Kim was in her room trying to write an essay during the fight.

At about 10 P.M. Steven told Sabrina that she was a jealous drama queen who also suffers from paranoia, and that once she calmed down she could call him, otherwise she

66

should leave him alone. Steven slammed out of the apartment and Sabrina yelled after him, "Come back! If you leave, I will hunt you down and make you regret every single word that you've said to me tonight, you nasty, cheating SOB." Steven left without saying another word to Sabrina. His body was found the next morning at 7 AM in Waterloo Park by a police patrol. He found Steven's body, along with his wallet, and called his roommate to inform him of the death. The motive was not robbery, as Steven's wallet and money were not touched. The cause of death was four stab wounds in the back. The estimated time of death was 2:30 A.M.

Trial

Clerk: Oyez, Oyez, Oyez. Anyone having business before the Superior Court of Justice attend now and you shall be heard. Long live the Queen! Please be seated.

Judge: Will the attorneys, the court clerk, and bailiff please take their places for the trial. Please bring in the accused Mr. Deputy. Order ladies and gentlemen. Please escort the jury in Mr. Deputy.

Clerk: Queen versus Gray.

Judge: Good morning. You are now instructed to give your complete attention to the evidence and arguments that are about to be presented. Remember that the accused pleads not guilty to the charge of first degree murder made against her. Your sole duty is to determine is her guilt or innocence. Mr. Green, are you ready for your opening statement?

Green: I am your honor.

Opening statements:

Green: Good morning ladies and gentlemen of the jury. My name is Chris Green and I am an assistant Crown Attorney. The accused has been charged with the crime of murder for the death of her boyfriend Steven Klein. I do not believe in lengthy arguments, and I let my witnesses do all the talking for me. Thus, I will keep this short and to the point. The Crown will prove that on the night of the murder the lovers argued, as they did frequently. After the argument, Steven left the accused's apartment and proceeded to bike around the neighborhood in order to cool off. During the night, while Steven was on his way home, the accused stabbed him four times in the back. The knife that the accused used to murder Steven was his own pocket knife. I am going to prove that the accused

68

intentionally and with predetermined thought did murder Steven Klein, who was one of the most liked and well-respected men among his friends and classmates. He was the recipient of many academic awards and scholarships. He was an outstanding student and friend and the evidence that I will present to you will show that Steven was murdered by the person he loved and trusted most.

There were witnesses that heard the couple fighting, and the knife with which Steven was murdered was found in the accused's bag. The accused was also heard taking a shower very late at night, as well as doing laundry. The idea behind the nightly cleaning spree was to eliminate any incriminating evidence, such as blood. When that seemed impossible, the accused attempted to get rid of the evidence by disposing of the clothes in a dumpster. The investigating officer was able to not only find the accused's clothing, but also prove that she was wearing them that night. The experts will tell you that the blood stains found on the accused's clothes match the blood of Steven Klein.

Ladies and gentleman of the jury, a young man has died much too soon before his time, and I will prove to you beyond a reasonable doubt, that this young lady sitting before you is guilty of this horrible crime. Thank you for your attention, as well as for your service to our country.

Judge: Mr. King we are ready for your opening arguments.

King: My name is Paul King and I represent Sabrina Gray in this murder case. Sabrina Gray is a young lady, who like many of us, experienced relationship difficulties; however, she is not a murderer. She has suffered profusely since the day that her boyfriend Steven was murdered. Sabrina and Steven have been together since grade 9; high school sweethearts who experienced many things together. They have been there for each other during both good times such as starting university and prom, as well as during not so good times, such as family sickness, death, and school stress. They have built their dreams together and their dreams were slowly coming true.

My question to you, ladies and gentleman of the jury is why would two people who love each other create dreams, make plans together, and have the desire to spend the rest of there lives together, destroy what is obviously important to them, and murder the person that they love? I will present evidence to you that will prove that this young lady sitting before you is not guilty of the crime.

First of all, did anyone actually seen Sabrina commit this horrific crime? No. The murder weapon that was said to be found in the accused's bag was Steven's pocket Swiss Army Knife, one of several that he owned and gave to Sabrina to keep. There are hundreds of such knives out there that are exactly the same as the murder weapon, and many young university students possess them. I will also prove to you that the clothes that Sabrina wore that night had Steven's blood on them from an earlier kitchen accident. Earlier in the evening Steven and Sabrina were cooking, and Steven cut himself. Sabrina used her shirt to stop the flow of blood – this the reason for which Steven's blood happened to be on her shirt. When she discovered that the blood stains could not be removed she disposed of the clothes.

I ask you, ladies and gentlemen of the jury, to listen with open minds to all of the evidence presented to you, and I strongly believe that once you have heard all the evidence, you like I, will know beyond a reasonable doubt that this young lady before you is not the person who killed Steven Klein. Thank you.

Green: Your Honour, there are certain facts that are agreed upon. They are as follows:

Stevens Klein's teachers, coaches, as well as friends, have given statements that prove that Steven Klein was well-liked. Jim Thomson is a deputy with the Waterloo Regional Police Department. He was the first one on the scene. Steven did cut himself during dinner, the night before his death. The bag and clothes that were found in the dumpster do belong to Sabrina Gray. Sabrina Gray and Steven Klein were together since high school. The walk from Sylvie's Bar that is located on Columbia and King is within a 25 minute walking distance from where Stevens Klein's body was found. The time of death of Steven Klein was estimated at 2:30 A.M.

Judge: Thank you Mr. Green. Does the Crown wish to present any witnesses at this time?

Green: The Crown calls Kim Wild to the stand.

Judge: Will the clerk please swear in the witness.

Clerk: Do you want to swear on the Bible or affirm?

Kim: The Bible.

Clerk: Do you solemnly swear that the testimony you are about to give in this case is the truth, the whole truth, and nothing but the truth, so help me God?

Kim: I swear to speak the truth.

Green: For the record, what is your full name?

Kim: Kimberly Wild.

Green: How long have you known the accused?

Kim: Since September 2003.

Green: How long have you been living with the accused?

Kim: Since September, so about 10 months.

71

Green: During the time you and Sabrina have lived together, had Steven Klein been a frequent visitor?

Kim: Yes, Steven spent most of the days at our apartment, and most weekends he would stay over.

Green: Would you say that Steven and Sabrina were a happy couple, or did they spend much time arguing?

Kim: I don't know; they seemed happy, but they also argued a lot as well.

Green: On average, how often would they argue?

Kim: Maybe once a week.

Green: Who was the one starting the arguments, and what were they mostly about?

Kim: It was usually Sabrina who would start the argument, and mostly it was about the same thing. Sabrina was very jealous of Steven, and she would accuse him of cheating on her, or not spending enough time with her.

Green: On the night of Steven's death, did the couple argue?

Kim: Yes.

Green: What about?

Kim: Sabrina was accusing Steven of cheating on her.

Green: Was the fight a typical argument?

Kim: Well, this time it sounded like Sabrina was really upset, and that she actually had proof of Steven cheating on her. She was very upset.

Green: How long did the couple argue?

Kim: They argued for about an hour, after which Steven left.

Green: What did Sabrina do after Steven left?

Kim: She cried, called him names, and said that she was going to kill him for being unfaithful.

Green: What were Sabrina's exact words when she spoke of hurting Steven?

Kim: I am not sure of the exact word by word quotation, but she said something like this: "No man will ever cheat on me and get away with it. I will kill all those that even toy with the idea of cheating, so I will just have to kill him, I guess."

Green: Did she say anything else?

Kim: I do not think so.

Green: What were some of the names that Sabrina called Steven?

Kim: SOB, cheater, and many others.

Green: What else did Sabrina do that night?

Kim: She stormed around the apartment, and than she grabbed her keys and left.

Green: What time did she leave, and did she say where she was going?

Kim: I'm not sure exactly what time it was when Sabrina left; it was after 11 P.M. for sure, because my watch beeped at 11 and I heard her leave after that. I was in my room, and Sabrina did not come in to tell me where she was going; she just left.

Green: What did you do after she left?

Kim: I finished reading, and got ready for bed.

Green: Do you know when Sabrina came in?

Kim: It was late at night. She woke me up, but I didn't check my watch to see what time it was.

Green: What did you hear?

Kim: I heard her walk in, drop some stuff in her room, and get in the shower.

Green: How did she seem the next morning?

Kim: Normal, she didn't seem upset anymore, just her usual self.

Green: Did she talk about Steven at all?

Kim: No, she just ate breakfast and watched TV. She never mentioned anything about Steven.

Green: Was it usual behavior after a fight?

Kim: Usually she tried to call him as soon as she got up, regardless if they had argued or not.

Green: But not this time?

Kim: No.

Green: How did Sabrina react when she found out that Steven was dead?

Kim: She kept saying that it couldn't be true. He didn't die.

Green: Was she upset?

Kim: I'm not sure; she stayed in her room for most of the day, and I didn't really see that much of her for the next few days.

Green: No more questions your honor.

Judge: Does the defense wish to cross-examine the witness?

King: Yes we do your honor. During the evening of Sabrina and Steven's argument, did you actually speak with Sabrina?

Kim: No, I was in my room the entire time.

King: How can you claim that Sabrina was more upset than usual?

Kim: Even after Steven left, I could hear her calling him names.

King: But you didn't actually see her, did you?

Kim: No.

King: So, you have actually no idea where Sabrina went, or what she took with her, or even what she wore to go out?

Kim: No.

King: Was it the first time that Sabrina took a shower during the night, before she went to bed?

Kim: No, she usually showered before she went to bed.

King: How close were you and Sabrina?

Kim: Well, we were roommates, we talked, went out together sometimes, and overall, got along.

King: But you and Sabrina were not actually close friends?

Kim: I guess we weren't close.

King: Did Sabrina ever confide in you?

Kim: No.

King: So how can you say how she felt the next morning, if Sabrina did not confide in you?

Kim: I just said what I saw.

King: After Sabrina found out about Steven's death, you did not see her for a few days?

Kim: That's correct.

King: So she could have been grieving?

Kim: Yes.

King: And you did not check on her even once?

Kim: No.

King: Have you seen this knife before?

Kim: Yes; it was Steven's.

King: Did you see it the night before the murder?

Kim: No, I was in my room most of the evening.

King: So you don't know if Steven left the knife at Sabrina's apartment, or if he had it with him?

Kim: No.

King: Did he ever leave his things at Sabrina's?

Kim: Yes, many times.

King: So he could have left that knife in Sabrina's bag?

Kim: Yes, I guess.

King: So, because you were in your room all night, you did not see what Sabrina wore to go out that night?

Kim: No.

King: Did you see Steven cut himself while preparing dinner?

Kim: No.

King: So you never saw or spoke to Sabrina the night of the argument?

Kim: No.

King: No more questions your honor.

Judge: Any further witnesses?

Green: Yes your honor. The people would like to call Mark Tyler to the stand.

Judge: Will the clerk please swear in the next witness.

Clerk: Do you want to swear on the Bible or affirm?

Mark: The Bible.

Clerk: Do you solemnly swear that the testimony you are about to give in this case is the truth, the whole truth, and nothing but the truth so help me God?

Mark: I do so swear.

Green: For the record, state your full name, and your relationship to the deceased.

Mark: My name is Mark Tyler and Steven was one of my best friends as well as my roommate.

Green: How long have you known Steven?

Mark: Since high school, so I guess almost 10 years.

Green: Have you known Sabrina the same amount of time?

Mark: Yes. Steven and Sabrina have been together since grade 9.

Green: So you have been close to both Steven and Sabrina?

Mark: Yes, Sabrina was my best friend's girlfriend.

Green: Can you tell me when you saw Steven for the last time?

Mark: We both wrote an exam earlier in the day. Afterwards, we came home and there was a message from Sabrina asking Steven to call her.

Green: What time was that at?

Mark: That was at about 5 P.M.

Green: Then what happened?

Mark: Steven called Sabrina, and spoke to her for about 5 minutes. When he finished talking with her, he came into the kitchen and told me that he was going over to Sabrina's for dinner and to talk about something with her. I asked him what it was that Sabrina wanted to discuss, and Steven said, "I don't know, but whatever it is, I am not sure if I want to hear it". I asked him if she was still upset about Steven studying with Jill.

Green: Who is Jill?

Mark: She's a student in our business class, and we worked on several assignments together and studied for a couple of tests together.

Green: Okay, go on.

Mark: Steven said that he thought that Sabrina had gotten over it, but now it was apparent she had not. I asked Steven if he was coming home that night, and he said that he was not sure. "I'll just call you once I know", is what Steven said.

Green: Then what happened?

Mark: Steven left; he biked over to Sabrina's house.

Green: Did he ever call you?

Mark: Yes, he called me at about 11:30 P.M. to tell me what happened.

Green: What did he say?

Mark: He told me that he was coming home that night after he had biked around and cooled down. He sounded very upset. He said that it was over between him and Sabrina. His exact words were: "She is crazy. She becomes more and more paranoid by the minute. I've had enough". Sabrina would not believe Steven that he and Jill just studied together. Sabrina accused Steven of cheating on her with Jill.

Green: How long did you and Steven speak for?

Mark: We were on the phone for about half an hour.

Green: Did Steven say what time he was going to come home at?

Mark: No; he said not to wait up for him because he really needed to cool off after the argument.

Green: To your knowledge, did Steven and Sabrina argue a lot?

Mark: Recently yes. For some reason, Sabrina felt very threatened by Jill, and she was becoming more and more suspicious of Steven.

Green: Did Steven typically go for bike rides after arguments with Sabrina?

Mark: Yeah, if not a bike ride, then a run, or he would go for a swim; he usually did do something athletic afterwards.

Green: So what did you do after you spoke to Steven?

Mark: I had a shower and went to bed.

Green: What happened in the morning?

Mark: I got up very early because I wanted to go for a run. I was surprised that Steven was not home.

Green: How did you know?

Mark: His shoes were missing, and the door to his bedroom was open. It's closed during the night when Steven goes to sleep.

Green: So you knew that he did not come home?

Mark: Yes.

Green: What happened then?

Mark: Before I left for my run, the police called and told me about his death.

Green: What did you do then?

Mark: I couldn't believe it, so I called Sabrina to see if she knew anything.

Green: What did Sabrina say when you told her?

Mark: She said that she didn't give rat's ass as to what happened to that SOB. She also said that it served him right, for all the cheating he did on her. She also said that his death is really a service to the human race, since the virus got removed. .

Green: Was that a typical reaction after an argument?

Mark: No, usually, she was the one calling him and apologizing and asking Steven to forgive her. This time, she sounded not happy, but as if being killed was the right punishment.

Green: So when you spoke to her she didn't sound upset or surprised about Stevens's death?

King: Objection your Honor! Leading the witness

Judge: Please rephrase the question.

Green: When you spoke to Sabrina, how did she sound?

Mark: She sounded angry perhaps, but not upset or surprised.

Green: No more questions your honor.

Judge: Does the defense wish to cross-examine the witness?

King: Yes your honor. How long have you and Steven known Jill?

Mark: For about one year.

King: How often would you and Steven study with Jill?

Mark: Fairly often since we were taking the same classes.

King: Before your last exam, the one that you, Jill and Steven wrote the day before he died, did you study with Steven and Jill?

Mark: I did for an hour or so, and then I left.

King: Where did you go?

Mark: Home.

King: What about Steven?

Mark: He stayed.

King: Where were you studying?

Mark: At Jill's.

King: Does she have any roommates?

Mark: No, she lives by herself.

King: So once you left, Steven and Jill were alone. Did Steven come home that night?

Mark: No, not really. He came home in the morning.

King: So he spent the night at Jill's.

Mark: Yes, they pulled an all-nighter.

King: Is that all?

Mark: Yes, I do believe so. Steven would never cheat on anyone, especially not Sabrina. Whatever problems they had, he cared about her. She also told him multiple times that no one ever cheated on her, and she would personally kill anyone who would do that to her. Steven would laugh at of and say that the same goes for him.

King: What about Jill. Did she act as if she wanted to be with Steven?

Mark: Many times; she send Steven notes and invitations to parties or get-togethers, but Steven always made it very clear that he was not interested.

King: Did Steven, say anything about the study session with Jill, after he came home?

Mark: No, not really.

King: How did Steven behave when he come back from Jill's?

Mark: He looked very tired, and was distracted. He did not want to talk, but just said that it was a long night.

King: Do you think that Jill was capable of making a sexual pass at Steven?

Mark: Maybe, I really don't know.

King: Do you think that when Jill did not get her way with Steven, she would take it out on him for humiliating her?

Mark: I do not know.

King: How did Jill seem during the exam?

Mark: We did not really see her. She came in late, and sat at the back of the room. She left before Steven and I were done.

King: Have you ever seen Jill when she was angry at someone?

Mark: Yes.

King: How did she act, and what was it about?

Mark: We were talking together, Steven Jill and myself in the library one time, when this one guy came in to the library. When Jill saw him, she jumped up, and started shouting at him, and when he tried to say something she hit him. Steven and I grabbed her and sat her down so that she would cool down. That was when she told us that he stood her up, and did not show up for their date. Then she started crying, and that was really that.

King: Did she ever lash out at Steven that way?

Mark: No

.King: Thank you your honor.

Judge: Any further witnesses for the Crown?

Green: Yes Your Honour, the Crown would like to call Dr. Scott Bauer.

Clerk: Do you want to swear on the Bible or affirm?

Bauer: The Bible.

Clerk: Do you solemnly swear that the testimony you are about to give in this case is the truth, the whole truth, and nothing but the truth so help me God?

Bauer: I swear.

Green: Your Honor I would ask that Dr. Bauer be qualified as an expert in blood splatter analysis. I can advise the court that his expertise is not in dispute.

Judge: Is this the case Mr. King?

King: Agreed Your Honour.

Green: Dr. Bauer, could you state your occupation for the record?

Bauer: I am a forensic specialist, and I specialize in the areas of blood splatter analysis and DNA testing.

Green: How long have you worked in your profession?

Bauer: For about 12 years.

Green: This would mean that you have much experience in blood splatter analysis and DNA testing?

Bauer: Yes, I would say that I have experience in that area.

Green: Could you tell us more about the blood splatter test.

Bauer: Yes. The purpose of the test is to determine if the pattern of blood spray on a piece of clothing has been caused by a weapon fired and what kind of weapon, etc. Basically, when there is a wound blood is spilled, and depending on what has caused the wound, there will be a different pattern that the blood creates. The pattern is determined by the weapon that has been used to inflict the wound, as well as the distance of the weapon from the body. In this case the weapon was a knife which left a specific pattern of blood that was typical to that instrument.

Green: Have you examined the bloodstains on Sabrina's shirt?

Bauer: Yes.

Green: Do they match Steven's blood?

Bauer: Yes.

Green: Does the pattern on Sabrina's shirt match the pattern that is left after a stabbing someone?

Green: In this case there is a pattern on Sabrina's shirt that would match multiple stabbings. However, there is more blood present on the shirt that would be normally present after four stab wounds.

Green: Are you saying that the pattern is there, but there is also additional blood on the shirt?

Bauer: Yes.

Green: No more questions Your Honour.

Judge: Would the defense like to cross-examine the witness?

King: Yes, Your Honour. Dr. Bauer, you have said that the pattern on Sabrina's shirt matches the typical pattern of a knife wound, but that there also is extra blood and another pattern? Is that correct?

Bauer: Yes, there is the typical pattern of a stabbing, and the blood on the shirt matches the blood of the deceased, but there are other stains on the shirt that match the blood type of the deceased.

King: The evening before Steven died he cut himself with a knife and Sabrina used her shirt to stop the blood. Could the patterns on the shirt be from Sabrina stopping the blood?

Bauer: As I have said there is more blood on the shirt than there should be, which means that scenario could have happened.

King: Could the pattern perhaps be solely caused by the kitchen incident?

Bauer: No. The extra blood could be from the kitchen incident, but the other pattern is unmistakable - it comes from a knifing.

King: Have you ever been wrong?

Bauer: Rarely.

King: But there were cases that you made mistakes on with your analysis?

Bauer: Yes, there were a few cases where I was wrong.

King: No more questions Your Honour.

Green: The Crown rests Your Honour.

Judge: Will the defense please call their first witness.

King: The defense calls Amanda Moss.

Judge: Will the clerk please swear in the witness.

Clerk: Would you like to swear on the Bible or affirm?

Amanda: The Bible.

Clerk: Do you solemnly swear that the testimony you are about to give in this case is the truth, the whole truth, and nothing but the truth so help me God?

Amanda: I swear.

King: Would you state your whole name and your occupation for the record?

Amanda: My name is Amanda Moss, and I am a bartender at Sylvie's Bar.

King: How long have you been working at that bar?

Amanda: For the past 2 years.

King: Were you working on the night of Thursday, May 13?

Amanda: Yes I was.

King: What time did you start work?

Amanda: At 7 P.M.

King: What time did you work until?

Amanda: Until 3 A.M.

King: Was the bar busy that night?

Amanda: No not really, the busy nights are Wednesdays and Saturdays, not Thursdays.

King: Did you see the accused, Sabrina Gray, at the bar that night?

Amanda: Yes, I did.

King: What time did she come in?

Amanda: It was about midnight. I had just returned from my break, when this young woman ordered a drink from me.

King: How did she look to you?

Amanda: Distressed; it looked like she was crying.

King: Do you remember what clothes the accused wore?

Amanda: She had on a pink tank top that was stained, and jeans.

King: What did the stain on the defendant's tank top look like to you. What do you think it was?

Amanda: I am not sure, maybe blood.

King: Can you describe what it looked like?

Amanda: It covered the lower half of her shirt. It was dark, and really looked like something was spilled on it. Actually, it is very hard to describe it. However, this is the best description that I can give you.

King: How often did the accused come over to buy drinks that night?

Amanda: At least 3 more times after the first drink.

King: When did you see her for the last time?

Amanda: At exactly one minute before 2:00 she came to the bar to get her last drink. It was a shot, so she drank it fast, and I saw her leave a few minutes after that.

King: Where is your bar located?

Amanda: On King and Columbia.

King: How long do you think it takes to walk from your bar to Waterloo Park?

Amanda: Roughly 20 to 25 minutes.

King: Ladies and gentlemen, it takes about 20 to 25 minutes to walk from that bar to the park, and Steven was killed at about 2:30. That leaves the accused only 5 to 10 minutes to find him in the park, where she did not know that he was and kill him. I do not think that this is physically possible. Thank you

Judge: Does the Crown wish to cross-examine the witness?

Green: Yes Your Honor.

Green: How sure are you that the stain on Sabrina's shirt was blood?

Amanda: It looked like blood, but I am not sure.

Green: How strong is the light where you stand?

Amanda: It is not that strong, There is only one light, and that is in the centre.

Green: Where do you stand in relationship to the light?

Amanda: To the left of it.

Green: From there you are sure you can determine that someone's shirt is stained with blood, or is even stained at all?

Amanda: I am not sure what it was.

Green: So it could have been the light reflecting on her shirt that created the illusion of a stain.

Amanda: Maybe.

Green: You have said that it takes 20 to 25 minutes to walk to Waterloo Park. How long does it take when you take the shortcut?

Amanda: I am not sure, I never take the shortcut.

Green: How often do you walk from your bar to Waterloo Park?

Amanda: Never really.

Green: So how can you say that it takes 20 to 25 minutes to walk that distance?

Amanda: From looking at the distance, it seems like a 20 to 25 minute walk.

Green: But you are not absolutely sure, are you?

Amanda: No.

Green: Thank you Your Honor.

Judge: Any further witnesses?

King: No Your Honor, the defense is resting.

Judge: Mr. Prosecutor are you ready to proceed to your closing arguments?

Green: Yes Your Honor.

Closing Arguments

Green: Ladies and gentlemen of the jury I am delighted to have the opportunity to speak to you once again. All through this trial you have been attentive and I would like to thank you for your participation on behalf of the Crown. Similar to many other murders, this murder occurred in the dead of night without witnesses present. Even though there may not have been any witnesses to the murder, the individuals who did speak to you made it clear that it was Sabrina Gray who committed the murder. First of all, the couple argued in the night before the murder, and Sabrina's jealous nature has been shown very clearly. Since most murders occur between people that love each other, this murder is not an exception. Sabrina's jealousy was the motive and the fight was the trigger that gave this young woman the strength to kill the person that she loved. Sabrina's shirt was stained perhaps when she was at the bar; however, there was no clear evidence given; the blood stained Sabrina's shirt for sure after she left the bar. So Sabrina could have walked out of Sylvie's bar, taken the shortcut to the park, found Steven, since she knows the route that he takes to go home, and stabbed him there.

You may be asking yourself, how did she know where Steven would be? She knew his route home, since they both took it many times; she knew his pattern of behavior, from being with him for so many years. Thus, it was not hard for her to find Steven that night. Fueled by alcohol, jealousy, and her sense of injustice, she set out to deliver justice. The justice was delivered in the form of four stab wounds, which were deadly to the young man.

I have every faith that when you retire to the jury room to deliberate, you will look at the facts with open minds, and on that basis find the accused guilty of first degree murder. Thank you.

Judge: Thank you Mr. Green. Mr. King, are you ready to present your closing arguments?

King: Yes your honor. Ladies and gentlemen of the jury, I stand before you once again to restate to you my previous convictions and beliefs. This young lady before you may be guilty of arguing with Steven and being suspicious of Steven, but she is not guilty of murdering the person that she loved for so many years. As you all know, disagreements occur among people that love each other; it is simply a fact of life that people who know each other really well and love one another argue, and may not always see eye to eye. However, arguments between lovers do not mean that one lover will murder their partner.

Sabrina and Steven were a young couple, who after their argument, needed time to cool off and they both proceeded to do so in their own ways. Steven went biking, while Sabrina went to a bar. As a matter of fact, she was so distracted and distraught that she did not even notice that the shirt that she was wearing was stained with Steven's blood. She left the house in exactly the same clothes that she was wearing during the day, because she simply needed to clear her mind. She went to Sylvie's where she behaved like many of her peers do: she had a few drinks, danced, listened to music and once the bar was closed she proceeded to go home. At the time she left, and taking into consideration the distance from the bar to the Park where Steven was murdered, it is not possible to make it in such a short period of time. Even if Sabrina took a short cut it is impossible that she would know exactly where Steven was. Even knowing his typical route home, she wouldn't know that he was still out in the park. I have full confidence that you will consider these discrepancies while you are deliberating, and after careful review of the facts, you will find this young lady not guilty of the murder of Steven Klein. Thank you.

Judicial instructions:

Judge: Ladies and Gentlemen of the jury, you have heard all the evidence in this case, and now it is the time for you to deliberate. Sabrina Gray has been charged with murder of the first degree. In order for you to find her guilty of first-degree murder the following needs to be true.

- Murder is first-degree murder when it is planned and deliberate.

- Without limiting the generality of subsection (2), murder is planned and deliberate when it is committed pursuant to an arrangement under which money or anything of value passes or is intended to pass from one person to another, or is promised by one person to another, as consideration for that other's causing or assisting in causing the death of anyone or counselling another person to do any act causing or assisting in causing that death.

- Irrespective of whether a murder is planned and deliberate on the part of any person, murder is first degree murder when the victim is
    - a police officer, police constable, constable, sheriff, deputy sheriff, sheriff's officer or other person employed for the preservation and maintenance of the public peace, acting in the course of his duties;
    - a warden, deputy warden, instructor, keeper, jailer, guard or other officer or a permanent employee of a prison, acting in the course of his duties; or

- o   a person working in a prison with the permission of the prison authorities

- Irrespective of whether a murder is planned and deliberate on the part of any person, murder is first degree murder in respect of a person when the death is caused by that person while committing or attempting to commit an offence under one of the following sections:

(*a*) section 76 (hijacking an aircraft);

(*b*) section 271 (sexual assault);

(*c*) section 272 (sexual assault with a weapon, threats to a third party or causing bodily harm);

(*d*) section 273 (aggravated sexual assault);

(*e*) section 279 (kidnapping and forcible confinement); or

(*f*) section 279.1 (hostage taking).

- Irrespective of whether a murder is planned and deliberate on the part of any person, murder is first degree murder when the death is caused by that person while committing or attempting to commit an offence under section 264 and the person committing that offence intended to cause the person murdered to fear for the safety of the person murdered or the safety of anyone known to the person murdered.

- Irrespective of whether a murder is planned and deliberate on the part of a person, murder is first degree murder when the death is caused while committing or attempting to commit an indictable offence under this or any other Act of Parliament where the act or omission constituting the offence also constitutes a terrorist activity.

- Irrespective of whether a murder is planned and deliberate on the part of a person, murder is first degree murder when the death is caused while committing or attempting to commit an offence under section 81 for the benefit of, at the direction of or in association with a criminal organization.

- Irrespective of whether a murder is planned and deliberate on the part of a person, murder is first degree murder when the death is caused while committing or attempting to commit an offence under section 423.1.

- All murder that is not first degree murder is second degree murder

Manslaughter: Culpable homicide that is not murder or infanticide is manslaughter.

Culpable: Deserving of blame or censure as being wrong, evil, improper, or injurious

Homicide: A person commits homicide when, directly or indirectly, by any means, he causes the death of a human being.

- Homicide is culpable or not culpable.
- Homicide that is not culpable is not an offence.
- Culpable homicide is murder or manslaughter or infanticide.
- A person commits culpable homicide when he causes the death of a human being,

(*a*) by means of an unlawful act;

(*b*) by criminal negligence;

93

(*c*) by causing that human being, by threats or fear of violence or by deception, to do anything that causes his death; or

(*d*) by willfully frightening that human being, in the case of a child or sick person.

Now that you have been instructed on the law, it is time for you to retire and finally be able to discuss the case.

Appendix B: Juror Survey

Please answer the following questions honestly.
Personal Information:
1. Age: _____

2. Gender (circle one):   Female   Male

3. Race:
Caucasian
Asian
Aboriginal
Latin
Black
Other
If other please state.

4. Religion:
Roman Catholic
Protestant
Christian
Jewish
Moslem
Other; please state_____

5. First language:
English
French
Other; please state_____

Occupation:
Student
Fully Employed

If you are a student, state your year of study (circle one):
1st 2nd   3rd   4th   5th

What is your major/majors of study?

Have you ever served on a jury?
Yes.
No.

6. Have you ever been in charge of a team, or a group, or a committee? For example, coordinator of a yearbook.
Yes.

No.

7. Have you enjoyed being in charge of others?
Yes.
No.

8. Do you enjoy organizing events?
Yes.
No.

9. Would you describe yourself as a:
Leader
Follower

10. Do you enjoy working in a group, towards a common goal, such as a group
    project?
Yes
No

11. When you work in a group, state your most frequent role. For example, note
    taker.

12. How would your best friend describe you as a person?

13. How would you describe yourself?

14. State the activities that you enjoy doing during your free time. Fore example,
    types of sports.

15. What is the job that you would like to have after you finish university?

16. Does it matter to you what your friends think about important world issues?
Yes.
No.

17. Do you like to be involved in
The community
Residence
School

18. If you have circled one or more of the above answers please list what you are
    involved in.

Appendix C: Results for Condition 1

Defense disengaged, Crown Neutral

Crown's opening statement.

During this time all ten jury members sat quietly in their seats, and most were waiting to hear what the lawyers had to say. Few jurors, mostly 9 and 7 sipped coffees and only juror number 8 leaned closer to the screen to take in all the information given to them by the Crown. The others listened, and occasionally shifted in their seats.

Defense opening arguments:

During the opening remarks given to the jury by the defense, there was a little bit more activity happening among the jurors. Juror number 9 took his attention from the trial and looked around at the other jurors, who did not make eye contact with juror 9. Juror number 5 smirked at the defense's words, as well as rolled his eyes and had a disbelieving expression on his face. This was the only external emotional reaction shown by the jury to the remarks given by the lawyers. In addition, juror 7 cracked his neck during this time, and juror number1, similar to juror 9, looked around at the other jurors, but the others did not make eye contact with him.

First witness for the Crown:

When the first witness came in all the jurors were listening intently to the Crown's questioning and the answers provided by the witness. It was when the defense was cross-examining the witness that juror 3 started to look around, smiling, and looking very bored. This juror was clearly not being engaged by the defense examination of the witness. Juror 8, similar to 3, smiled when the defense was finished, and all through this

97

cross examination it was noticed that the jurors' attention was not captured by this lawyer.

Witness 2 for the Crown:

The jurors are following the questioning of the witnesses by the lawyers, and there is little activity happening. Juror number 4 is yawning, but is still listening to the testimony. Juror number 2, however, looks concerned during this witness's testimony, and appears to believe the witness. During the cross examination of the witness by the defense, jurors 3 and 7 look around, but they do not make eye contact with others, or with each other. Once this witness finished testifying, the first segment of the trial was finished. It was time for the first break, and a chance for the jury members to talk with each other, and get to know one another. The jury members had ten minutes to talk freely about any topic they liked, except the trial.

Break:

The jurors took this time to introduce themselves to each other and talk about very general topics. First, jurors 4 and 5 waved hello to one another; they appeared to recognize each other. Other jurors, mainly jurors 1, 9, 6, and 10, shake hands. Juror 1 goes to jurors 9 and 6 to shake hands. This juror also shakes hands and introduces himself to jurors 4, 3, and 2. Thus, during this brief time, jurors have introduced themselves to one another by name, and now are starting to exchange comments and laugh at each other's jokes. All the jury are still not very comfortable with each other; they are only beginning the process of learning about one another.

It has been observed that jurors 10 and 2 have a quick word with one another, and juror 10 jokes about this being his first jury duty. Juror number 7 addresses everyone, and asks the year of study of all the jury members. This juror is trying to learn more about the other members of this jury. Jurors 2 through 6 reply and share with the others their academic programs. Since all jurors are university students, the first conversations are about school, courses, and professors. This topic is a common among all the jury. They all recognize this, and embark on exchanging comments, questions, and ideas about school. Thus, jurors 4 and 5 talk with one another, and it should be recalled that those two jurors may have recognized each other from school.

Similarly, jurors 2 and 7 talk about shared classes and each other's understanding of course materials. Other jurors are listening to their conversation, and do not interrupt. Juror 10 talks again, and this time he engages jurors 9, as well as juror 2 in a conversation. Other jurors, specifically 4 and 5 speak up. There is discussion amongst the jurors. It has been noted that jurors 2 and 10 have the qualities of leaders. They lead and start many conversations, especially after lengthy silences that fall upon the group. These two jurors take the initiative to break the uncomfortable silences and fill them with small talk.

When a silence has fallen on the group, while juror 8 stretches, juror 10 asks a general question of the group about psychology. Juror 7 answers juror 10 and they talk about their education in psychology. In addition, jurors 1 and 2 start a conversation amongst themselves and jurors 3, 4, and 5 nod in response. They listen, but do not contribute to the discussion. While jurors 10 and 7 speak, juror 1 joins their conversation and talks about his psychology education. Juror 10 dominates the conversation, and is most comfortable speaking. This is apparent during another uncomfortable silence, which juror 10 breaks by asking about a midterm exam in a psychology course. Juror 2 answers and shares with others exam stories, especially one about a fire alarm. Juror 7 makes remarks to juror 2's story and juror 8 joins in. It is juror 2, however, who continues talking and engaging others in conversation. At this time, jurors 3, 4, and 5 talk to one another. While juror 6 is silent, juror 7 talks, and so do juror 3 and 4. These two jurors speak much together. At the same time, jurors 10, 2, and 8 also are engaged in conversation.

From this first break a few conclusions can be drawn. It is becoming apparent that juror 2 and 10 are leaders. These two jurors have started many conversations, broken uncomfortable silences, and engaged other jury members in conversations. Similarly, jurors 8 and 7 are also very involved in conversation with others, but they have spent much time speaking to jurors 2 and 10. Jurors 3, 4, and 5 seem to be happy talking together, and even though they join the conversation of others, they spend much time talking together. At the same time, jurors 6 and 9 are very silent, and not contributing much to any conversations. Juror 1 is a little bit more active than jurors 6 and 9, but not by much.

Therefore, after the conclusion of the first break, there are two promising leaders, and the beginnings of subgroups. In addition, the jurors have found common ground in the topic of school. All of them are students of the same institution, and take or have taken the same courses. This is the common thread among them.

Witness 3:

During this time, jurors turn their attention again to the screen and the trial. Juror 4 yawns visibly, and juror 5 looks around at others, without making eye contact. Juror 3 also glances around, but not much. The most activity during the Crown's presentation comes from jurors 4 and 5. Juror 4 continues to yawn, while 4 others are very attentive to the lawyers and witness's presentation.

During the cross-examination of the witness, not much action occurs. Juror 4 shifts in his seat, while juror 7 rubs his eyes. Juror 4 smirks at the testimony and than proceeds to tilt his head down in a way that he does not see the screen. Juror 5's reactions are the same, in that he also does not watch the screen and has his head down. During the next witness, not much action is observed, other than, juror 4 continuing to yawn and look tired. Thus, during this segment of the trial, jurors 4 and 5 have been most active, however, 4 was mostly looking tired and yawning. The other jurors have been listening to the testimony and did not appear to have visible reaction to the witnesses or the lawyers.

Break 2:

Another 10 minute break is announced. Jurors have another break during which they can continue to get to one another better and strengthen their connections. At first juror 2 smirks, but no one speaks. The silence is interrupted by juror 1 asking all the other jurors about their major of study. Jurors 7, 8, 3, and 4 reply and start talking. Juror 10 interrupts the conversation about majors of study to ask juror 3 a question about a possible mutual acquaintance. Juror 10's questions seemed to have stopped the conversation, for a beat.

Juror 7, however, is the one to break the silence by asking a question of juror 9. Jurors 7 and 9 have a conversation together, and ask each other, or answer each other's questions in turn. While juror 6 does not contribute to the conversation, juror 10 had been listening to the conversation of juror 7, and 9 and joins them with a comment. Juror 7 asks a question of juror 1 in order to engage this person in a conversation, and learn a bit more about that person. Juror 7 is very talkative, and while this juror is describing a professor, juror 2, who is listening, looks incredulous. The small subgroup of 3, 4, 5, say nothing during this time, and 6 not only does not say anything and joins the others in conversations, but also looks very withdrawn. Jurors 10 and 7 enjoy a lively conversation about professors and school, while others especially 3, 4, 5, and 6 are silent. During the last moments of the break juror 2 speaks, while juror 5 makes a comment about juror 6 being half asleep. Before the break ends juror 10 asks one last question.

During this break jurors 7, 10 and 2 have been very active and have engaged others in general conversations. Jurors 2 and 10 continue to lead and have started many conversations; however, juror 7 has also been very active and has contributed much to many discussions. The major topic of conversation has been school. This seems to be the one topic that most jurors not only have in common, but are most comfortable talking about. This may stem from up-coming midterms which all the jurors will be writing.

Trial:

Crown rests, Defense first witness:

While the witness is sworn in, juror 5 laughs openly, while juror 4 shifts in his seat. After this, juror 5 seems to be asleep, while juror 2 smiles towards the end of the defense's questioning.

Cross examination:

At first juror 4 glances at juror 5, but juror 5 is looking down, and no eye contact is made. During this cross examination, juror 5 laughs at the cross examination.

Closing statements – Crown:

Not much activity is happening once again. It is juror 4 who shifts in his seat, and juror 5 who looks very tired.

During the closing remarks made by the defense, no activity was noted. Once the defense is finished, the judge gave the jurors their instructions. At this time, all jurors are looking up and listening to the judge. It is only juror 4 and 5 who shift in their seats, all the others are still. During this segment of the trial only juror 4 and 5 have been active. Juror 5 has mostly slept and laughed, while juror 4 has shifted much in his seat. This activity may not be important, since it may only have been an indication of the individual's restlessness. Other jurors however, have not engaged in any activities at all.

During this entire trial, there were very few activities that were visible. The jurors have not made eye contact, or reacted to testimonies of the witnesses. There were only a handful of reactions, but no visible body language that would suggest that jurors are connecting with one another, have silent communication, or are affected by the lawyers.

Deliberations:

The deliberations start with a silent vote for all the jurors. Once they all complete the task, they are informed that they have 20 to 30 minutes to discuss the case and vote openly on the verdict. The first task, however, is to select a foreperson. During the time that other jurors were finishing writing their silent vote, juror 3 and 4 were involved in conversation. Juror 10 is involved in discussion with juror 1, and 3 and 4 are laughing and talking together.

When everyone settles in to start discussing the case and selects a foreperson, jurors 3 and 9 make eye contact, everyone else is quiet. Juror 10 starts the discussion by asking "Who wants to be the foreperson, and also what exactly that is?" Juror number 7 responds and explains what the duties of a foreperson are. Juror number 2 speaks up and tells everyone that she has been a juror before. The group unanimously chooses her to be their foreperson. Thus, juror 2 becomes this group's foreperson. This juror has showed herself as a leader during the duration of the trial.

The foreperson asks everyone what they think, and encourages the group to talk. Juror 8 suggest going in a circle and have each person express their thoughts on the matter. The foreman disagrees at first, but juror 1 speaks up for the idea and it is agreed that they go in a circle and express their ideas.

Juror 10 starts by suggesting that the accused is not guilty and that evidence shown did not convince him. Juror 1 agrees with juror 10 that the accused is not guilty for the same reason - not enough evidence. Juror 9 remarks that the accused is guilty, but not of the first degree murder.

Before the other jurors can give their opinion juror 5 and 8 ask questions and a discussion begins. During this discussion juror 8 and 9 disagree. Following this, juror 1 asks another question, and so does juror 7. They are all relevant questions pertaining to the case. Juror 10 agrees with juror 7. Juror 10 also tries to get the group back on track, and leads the group back to the circle. Juror 6 gives his vote guilty, but this is not followed by an explanation or a reason.

The jurors continue, and state that the accused is guilty, but there is some doubt still. To this juror 3 nods. Another discussion occurs during which juror 10 agrees with juror 8's explanations of the blood splatter analysis and so does juror 5. Once this little discussion is over, juror 4 states that the accused is not guilty of first degree murder. After this declaration, another discussion starts up mainly about the difference between first and second degree murder. Jurors 1, 9, 8, and the foreperson are involved in this discussion. When juror 5 states that the accused is guilty, juror 7 asks juror 5 how that is possible. Juror 5 explains his reasoning, and juror 9 agrees with juror 5, however, juror 10 disagrees with jurors 9 interpretation of events.

During the discussion that follows, jurors 7 and 8 disagree with one another. Juror 8 is very involved in the discussions, and takes a dominating role. When juror 5 is trying to state his argument, juror 8 speaks up and discredits that juror's point. In the next discussion, jurors 7 and 10 agree with one another.

Juror 2, who is the foreperson, takes charge of the situation and gets the group focused on some of the evidence that was presented to the group, mainly the bloody clothes. She asks the group their opinions on this point, trying to get them focused on the evidence. A heated discussion ensued in which jurors 2, 7, 8, and 5 are involved. Juror 8 however, is taking a dominant role in this discussion. It is to juror 8's arguments that jurors 3, 4, 7 agree.

The conversation about the disposal of the bloody clothes continues and it is juror 5 this time, explaining his opinions, and convictions. While listening to juror's 5 story, jurors 3, 4 smiles, while juror 10 nods. Juror 3 makes a comment and juror 1 agrees. In the next conversation it is jurors 10 and 8 who are involved. Juror 8 talks and juror 10 agrees, and the foreperson nods. It is becoming clear that juror 8, who is very dominant, is leading the group even though he is not the foreperson. Juror 5 seem to disagree with 8 and presents counter arguments. To this it is jurors 3, 4, and 9 that agree. Juror 5 is not finished however, and continues the argument. Juror 3 continues to agree, and juror 7 joins in. Juror 8 tries to get a word in, but it is juror 7 who does. It is jurors 9 and 10 then, who contribute to the discussion, and juror 5 disagrees with juror 10's points. Jurors 8 and 9 talk over the other jurors and juror 9 disagrees with jury 8. At this time, even though the deliberations are not over, it should be noted that jurors 3 and 4 stick together, similar to at the breaks, and it is juror 8, 10, 2, and 7 who are very active during this time.

The foreperson is trying to lead the group in the discussion and have the group focus on the facts that they know about, in order to make sense of the evidence. It is juror 9 who starts talking, and juror 10 jumps in. Juror 8, who is very active, corrects juror 10 and continues the discussion. The foreperson joins in, and steers the conversation back to the facts. This time juror 5 speaks up, but juror 8 disagrees. The foreperson also disagrees with 8, and juror 10 is asking questions, and trying to make sense of the argument. Another little discussion ensues, but this time, about taking a vote and the time that the group has. The first open vote occurs, and the group is split. Jurors, 2, 6, 9, 5 and 4 vote guilty, while jurors 8, 3, 1, 10, and 7 vote not guilty.

The leaders are divided. Juror 2 and 10 were the two leaders when the deliberations began, and juror 8 joined them. Juror 8's comments throughout and active role during the discussions, have shown this juror's ability to lead and his interest in the case. At first jurors 3, 4, and 5 were together, or at least they spent much time speaking together, but during this first vote, juror 3 has supported the other jury members and not jurors 4 and 5. Jurors 8 and 9 have disagreed at times during the discussion, and after the vote they have taken different stands on the issue. Jurors 1 and 6 have not contributed much to the discussions, before and during the deliberations, but they have given the same vote of not guilty. During the prevote discussion, jurors 8 10 and 7 disagreed; however, during this first vote they have come to agree on the verdict.

The discussion continues, since the jurors are split in their decision. Juror 7 speaks up, and does not see how the accused could be guilty. To this the other jurors respond, and for a minute all speak at once. Juror 2, the foreperson agrees with 5, and they are supporting each others ideas. During the next conversation, when the jurors are discussing the same evidence once more, there is support for both guilty and not guilty. Jurors 2 and 8 disagree. They have voted differently. Juror 9 supports jurors 2; jurors 2 and 8 continue their discussion. Juror 5 supports juror 2 and juror 8 disagrees with juror 5. Juror 7 needs more evidence in order to be certain as to what happened. To this the foreperson tries to draw his attention to the expert witness testimony. Juror 8, however, is not convinced about the credibility of the expert witness, and juror 1 speaks up to side with juror 8.

The foreperson gets the group to take another vote. This time there is a small change. Juror 6 has changed his mind and is voting not guilty. This is most peculiar since this juror was not active during the trial or during deliberations. This one juror has been the most withdrawn and silent person in the group. What can be seen is that during the deliberations the leaders have split. Juror 2 was in one group and juror 10 was in another. In addition, a new leader emerged, or rather a juror, as equally active and involved in leading discussion during the deliberations as were the leaders. Since jurors 8 and 10 were each other's supporters, and have voted for the same verdict, the supporters of not guilty had two strong leaders. This may have contributed to juror 6's changing his mind, since two very strong leaders were arguing against only one leader. The other members of the jury were involved in defending and explaining their point of view, but the two strong voices together may have been stronger than one and convinced juror 6 to vote not guilty.

After this second vote jurors are explaining their choice of verdict. Jurors 7 and 10 support one another, and juror 4 expresses his concern. Jurors 9 and 7 speak up, but it is juror 3 who asks a question and looks at juror 5. The discussion continues and jurors 8 and 9 disagree. Jurors 2 and 9 continue to talk and support their side, but juror 10 is not convinced. Jurors 5 and 8 talk, but even though juror 2 joins in, juror 8 is not convinced. Jurors 5 and 8 continue to disagree, while juror 7 jokes about the evidence. Juror 5 does not see the joke, and does not believe that it is amusing.

The foreperson, states that it is a hung jury if that is the decision of the majority. Juror 5 continues to persuade others, but juror 8 does not seem to to like that. Jurors 7 and 10 question the evidence, and continue to support one another. Juror 9 answers the questions, and juror 10 reviews the evidence one more time. Jurors 7 and 8 are not convinced after the review of the facts. The foreperson asks the not guilty group about the kind of evidence that would convince them. Juror 7 replies. Jurors 5 and 7 continue to disagree, and juror 9 does not understand the arguments against the guilty verdict. It is juror 9 who asks the question of what would convince the others about changing their mind. It is jurors 7, 3, 4, who reply about a witness being discredited. The group continues to argue, but no one is changing their mind. Thus, after the final verdict, it is jurors 2, 5, 4, 9 who vote guilty and the rest vote not guilty.

During the first moments of the trial jurors 4 and 5 were the most active jurors. Much of their behavior was not important, but they showed the most reactions. In addition, during the breaks, they spent much time talking with one another, and 4's wave to 5 may have suggested a prior acquaintance. These factors may have contributed to these two jurors supporting each other during deliberations. The most puzzling behavior is that of juror 6 who did not speak much during the trial, as well as after. All the other jurors have talked to each other exchanged ideas and comments during the breaks. The verdict is surprising however, since during the trial the defense lawyer was very disengaged, while the Crown was neutral.

Appendix D: Results for Condition 2

Crown disengaged; Defense neutral.

Prior to the start of the trial, when everyone is looking around for seats and getting comfortable, jurors 1 and 9 talk. As the trial begins and all other jurors listen intently, juror 7 laughs, while jurors 8 and 2 look at one another and then around the room. When the defense steps in to deliver the opening statement, juror 8 takes notes, while juror 2 shifts in his seat. During this part of the trial juror 10 leans back to get more comfortable and continues to listen to the trial, while juror 2 looks puzzled. All of the other jurors have looked very intently at the trial, and given the trial their full attention. None of them looked at each other or was distracted by activity in the room.

The first break was announced and all jurors promptly began to talk. The time for the jurors to get to know one another has arrived, and they took the opportunity to do so. First, jurors 10 and 5 started talking to each other, while 7 and 2 talked and laughed. Juror 9 first introduced himself to juror 7 and then to the others. Juror 9 also asked all the jurors about the psychology course that they are taking. Juror 2 responded, and gave the group the name of the professor who was teaching his course. The group proceeded to talk about that section of the psychology course. Juror 9 continued talking with jurors 5 and 1. Juror 5 continued talking with juror 1, while 2 enjoyed a conversation with juror 3. Juror 9 continues talking with 7 and 2 about their psychology course. They find common grounds, by disliking the professor's tests and questions on them. Juror 9 also engages juror 1 in the discussion, and that juror contributes to the conversation. Juror 2 also has a quick word with juror 7.

While all this talking occurs, jurors 6, 4, 3, and 8 are silent and do not talk with anyone. While this group is not talking, juror 9 talks quite a bit, not only starting many discussions, but also dominating many of them. Jurors 5, 9, and 1 continue talking about psychology, and their likes and dislikes of the course. They have found a common bond. Juror 10 asks a question of all the other jurors about hockey. The jurors are working together to get to know one another, and the conversation shifts from school and common courses to sports.

Juror 9 is the first one to reply, and tells the others that he is a soccer fan and not a hockey one. Juror 9, even though, he is not a hockey fan, asks questions about the sport, and especially about the rules. Jurors 3 and 5 join in the conversation about hockey, and add their opinions. Juror 5 agrees with juror 9, and juror 5 continues talking about hockey. It is juror 9, however, who changes the topic to soccer. Juror 10 and 5 respond to juror 9's inquiries about their soccer interests, while jurors 6 and 8 are silent and aloof.

Jurors 8 and 1 were not involved in the sports conversation at all, but jurors 1 and 10 were listening and smiling, until juror 10 joined in. Jurors 3, 1, and 8, listen to jurors 9, 5, 2, and 7 talk, but only juror 1 joins in once in a while, the others listen and smile. Jurors 6, 8, 3, stay out of the conversations, especially juror 6. This juror has not been involved in any of the other conversations, and continues to sit aloofly and not contribute to the group's discussions. He is not inquiring about others' interests and not contributing his opinions or ideas. The other jurors who are silent, smile, or nod, or speak at times, while juror 6 is silent.

Juror 7 tells the others that he is from Las Vegas, Nevada. Juror 9 hears this and inquires about the sports that juror 7 has watched in the United States. Juror 7 explains that in the United States he watched mostly basketball. The jurors continue talking about sports and a small group emerges that not only watches sports, but agrees about hockey. This group involves jurors 10, 9, 1, 7, 3, and 5. Jurors 2 and 10 continue talking about sports, while 9 and 7 have another discussion about sports, aside from 2 and 10. Jurors 2 and 10 and 7 and 9 talk much together, laugh, and agree on many points. It is juror 9, however, who expresses his opinions the most, and continues to dominate the conversations. Jurors 6, 8, and 3 remain quiet, and do not talk with others. Juror 7 asks a question of juror 2, and they continue talking even when the break comes to an end. Before, the break has concluded jurors 3 and 4 join in, and contribute a comment here and there. Juror 8 not only does not talk, but spends his time during the break doodling on a piece of paper.

During this first break, juror 9 has shown his leadership skills by starting conversations, speaking with other jurors, and being very comfortable among strangers. He has led many conversations, and was able to engage other jurors in them. There was not a second of uncomfortable silence, since the time was filled with many conversations of which juror 9 was a part. Just as juror 9 has been very talkative, juror 6 was very quiet, and stood apart from the others. This juror did not try to learn more about his fellow jury members, and would not let the others learn about him. Juror 8 was similar, but not as standoffish as juror 6. Jurors 7, 2, 10, and 9 spoke most often, and engaged the other jurors in their discussions. Juror 4, although silent at first, joined in toward the end of the break.

While the trial begins again, juror 8 looks down at his doodle, while juror 2 looks around, but does not make eye contact with anyone. Juror 6 looks very tired, and is fighting sleep. This may be the reason for which juror 6 is not very involved in the discussions. As the testimony continues, juror 3 yawns, and juror 4 looks very bored and uninterested. Juror 2, however, listens with much concentration, and furrows his brow at the witness's testimony. There are not many reactions during the trial.

Juror 8 takes notes, during the witness's cross-examination, while juror 6 plays with his name tag. Juror 5 leans back and tries to get more comfortable in his seat, while juror 3 is starting to lose interest in the trial and looks away from the screen. Juror 2 takes his eyes from the trial, and takes a look around the room. Jurors 1 and 3 copy him and do the same. Juror 3 yawns again, and juror 7 coughs and juror 6 looks puzzled first, and then proceeds to chew his nails. Juror 3 continues not to be interested in the proceedings, and so does juror 6. Juror 5, however, leans forward during the testimony of the Crown's witness. Juror 3 looks everywhere, but at the screen.

The trial continues and the expert witness takes the stand. Juror 6 yawns, and continues not to be impressed by, or interested in, the trial. Jurors 2 and 4 are trying to get more comfortable in their seats, but they continue watching the trial. Juror 10 looks down and yawns, while juror 3 looks around, rubs his eyes and looks about to fall asleep. Juror 2 yawns as well. The Crown rests, and another break is announced.

During the trial, most reactions of the jurors were nonverbal and involved looking bored and tired. Most were not interested in the proceedings, and some looked like they were going to fall asleep. Most did not look impressed, or very involved in the trial. The lawyers were also not making an effort to draw the jurors in, and as a result, the jurors were bored, confused, and uninterested.

The break began, and jurors 7 and 2 make a comment and laugh. Juror 6 also laughs, while he is looking around at the others. Juror 9 asks a question of the group, and jurors 5 and 7 promptly reply. Jurors 5 and 9 talk together, while the others are silent. Juror 9 continues to talk, and jurors 7 and 2 are having a conversation together. Jurors 5 and 9 talk together, and discover that they have a common background. They have gone to the same school in the past and know the same people. The rest of the jurors are silent during this exchange, and juror 2 smirks at the conversation that 5 and 9 are having. Jurors 7 and 2 laugh and break the silence. Juror 1 talks about having leftover turkey. This is right after Thanksgiving, and juror 1 yearns for turkey.

Juror 9 asks another question of juror 7 and once again dominates the conversation. This juror has much to say, on many topics, and does so without restraint. Juror 3 joins the conversation, and the conversation turns to food, and especially turkey. Jurors 9 and 7 pick up the conversation and continue talking about turkey, and juror 2 joins them. Juror 7 starts talking about commercials, but this topic does not catch the interest of the others, and the conversation shifts back to school. Juror 2 asks the group about their year of study, and all reply. Jurors 4 and 3 talk about their background, and juror 5 asks juror 4 where he is from. Juror 9 does not stay out of the conversations and talks as much as ever. Juror 5 talks about journalism program at Carlton, and juror 9 proceeds to talk about his background. Juror 9 continues talking, while jurors 6 and 8 are silent and uninvolved. Jurors 7 and 2 laugh and juror 2 shares with them his background. He has transferred from a business program. Juror 9 picks up the thread and jurors 2 and 9 talk about the business program.

During this break, not much has changed from the first break. Jurors 9, 7, 2, and 5 were very dominant, but juror 9 continued to be the leading voice during the discussions. Juror 4 spoke, but mostly when spoken too. Jurors 1 and 3 were involved here and there, but not much. They shared in the common laughter and made a comment once in a while. Jurors 10, 6, and 8 were as uninvolved as ever. They mostly stayed out of the conversations, especially jurors 8 and 6.

The break is over, and all of the jurors turn their attention to the trial once more. The first defense witness takes the stand, and juror 8 takes notes. The other jurors are silent, and are listening intently. During the cross examination of the witness, juror 4 is restless, and juror 3 is bored and plays with his name tag.

At the beginning of the closing statements jurors 3, 2, 10, and 7 start out listening to the lawyer', but they soon lose interest and 3, 2, and 10, start looking around appearing very restless. Juror 7 bites his nails all through the proceedings. When the defense takes the stands to give the closing argument, there is little action. Juror 3 stares in to space, and is not attentive, while jurors 2, 7, 5, and 1 laugh when the defense lawyer slips up in their speech. This group of jurors was listening, and did not miss the small, but important slip up. Juror 6 chews his nails, while juror 4 checks his watch. The trial is almost over, and it is the judge who informs the jurors on the deliberations proceedings. During this time jurors 7 and 1 look away, while juror 8 takes notes. The trial is over and jurors give their silent votes.

During the trial, many of the jurors were bored and uninterested, but juror 8, even though he was not involved in the group discussions at the breaks, took notes at different points during the trial. Juror 6 however, was as interested in the trial as ever. Jurors 3, 4, and 2, yawned much during the trial and looked around, yet there was no eye contact between the jurors. While jurors are writing their vote on a piece of paper, jurors 2 and 9 joke together, and juror 2 engages juror 5 in a conversation. Jurors 3 and 4 have a quick conversation, and so do jurors 9 and 1. The voting is over, and it is time for the jurors to elect a foreperson.

Deliberations begin, and juror 9 talks, while juror 8 asks questions, which are not related to the discussion at hand. Juror 3 brings them back to the topic at hand. It is jurors 9, 5, 7, and 2 who speak in favor of juror 4. Juror 4 is in legal studies and the group feels that this is important for the role of the foreperson. As a result, juror 4 becomes the group's foreperson. It is interesting, since juror 4 did not demonstrate strong leadership skills during the duration of the trial. Similar to the first condition, in this second condition a leader is not selected, but a person with experience and knowledge of the Canadian legal system. In the first condition, the elected foreperson was a formal juror, and that gave him the edge over the others. In this case, juror 9 is a clear leader, but it is juror 4 who has the role of leading the group.

The deliberations begin with an open vote in order to establish everyone's position on the issue of the accused's guilt. Jurors 8, 9, 2, vote guilty of first degree murder. Jurors 1 and 3 vote second degree murder, while 10, 5, 6, 7, vote not guilty. Juror 4 is undecided, and wavers between guilty of second degree murder, and not guilty. The discussion is about to begin, especially because after the first vote there are three different opinions. The main split however, is between guilty and not guilty, after the first vote 6 jurors have voted guilty while 4 has voted not guilty. It is important to note that jurors 2 and 9 are in agreement, while 5 and 7 are in opposition to them. During group discussions, it was this group of four that had the most to say, and spent much time in conversation with each other. During the first vote however, the group has split, and it is 2 and 9 verses 7 and 5. This is especially interesting since jurors 5 and 9 have a common background and friends. They have attended the same school in the past. This however, was not a strong enough bond to keep them together and cause them to have similar ideas. Juror 6, who did not speak and was not involved in the previous discussions, is voting not guilty, and the deliberations will show whether this juror will be able to contribute to the discussion, or whether he will continue looking tired and be withdrawn from the others.

The discussion starts with the foreperson, juror 4, asking juror 1 about why he chose second degree and not first. Juror 1 responds, and juror 9 interrupts and offers his opinion. Juror 9 also clarifies a point and the foreperson agrees with juror 9. Jurors 2, 5, and 8 agree with juror 9. The guilty voters are in agreement with one another so far. The foreperson leads the discussion by presenting the group with another important point to be considered by the group. The group listens to him. Juror 4, suggests that since the accused was drunk, it should be regarded as second degree murder. Juror 2 however, believes that being drunk signals intent, and those to jurors argue about this important point. Juror 9 speaks up and sides with juror 4, in thinking that the accused should be guilty of second degree murder. This juror is changing his mind slightly, since originally his vote was guilty of first degree murder. It appears that the argument between jurors 2 and 4 has made an impact on juror 9. Juror 5 speaks up for the not guilty verdict.

Juror 3 makes a comment, with which juror 9 disagrees; however, at that time, juror 5 comes in to argue for the not guilty side. Juror 5 suggests that it is important to look at the accused's attitude after the murder and juror 8 disagrees. Juror 9 joins in, and starts arguing the point with juror 8. They are in agreement, but juror 9 speaks loudly, and dominantly. Juror 9 suggests that the most important evidence is the blood. Juror 3 joins in, and agrees with juror 9. Juror 8 adds to what juror 9 and 3 were discussing, and so does juror 1. Juror 9 proceeds to sum up the discussion, by stating that the most important point and evidence is the blood. During this exchange the two groups voting guilty of first degree and second degree murder have joined together and supported one another through the arguments. Juror 6 however, continues to remain silent, and not joining any group.

Juror 8 asks the non-guilty group why they believe that the accused is not guilty. Juror 10 answers, and juror 5 joins in, to argue the point and both jurors 10 and 5 are in agreement. Juror 9 argues for guilt, and brings up the stabbing of the victim to the discussion. Jurors 1, 3, add to juror 9's arguments, and so does juror 2, even when he is trying to make a joke out of it. The guilty supporters stand together, and are supporting each others' points. Juror 9 continues to lead the discussion, and reiterates his previous arguments loudly. Even though this juror is not the leader in the formal sense, he continues to dominate the discussions, and makes himself heard over the other jurors. Juror 4, even though he is the foreperson, does not possess such domineering skills.

Juror 7 disagrees with jurors 9 statements; however, juror 9 cuts juror 7 off by stating his own arguments. Jurors 3 and 9 look at the situation from another angle, and concede that perhaps the murder was an accident. Juror 8 agrees with them that it could be a possibility. The discussion continues and jurors 8, 9, and 1 argue their points, and

118

stand united in the guilty verdict. Juror 5 disagrees with them, and juror 8, 9, 1, and 3 argue again. Jurors 8 and 9 continue talking and giving their arguments.

From this discussion, it is clear that these jurors who believe in the guilt of the accused, not only support each other, but argue together and support each others' arguments. They present a united front and work as a group to convince the others. Even though juror 9 is the loudest, and speaks the most, which could be seen as a leading role, all others speak, and give their opinions.

The not guilty group is much different in this respect. Juror 5 argues, and appears to be the leader for this group, but he gets very little support from his supporters. Up until this point, only jurors 7 and 10 have spoken up and contributed to the discussion; however, it was not in the same united manner as the guilty group. Juror 6 remains silent, and does not support his group members in their stands. Thus, when the second vote occurs, the two guilty groups join, and vote guilty of second degree murder. These jurors are 1, 2, 3, 4, 8, and 9. The not guilty jurors are 5, 6, 7, and 10. After the first set of discussions, juror 4 has made up his mind fully and is voting guilty. The others votes have remained the same.

The discussion starts again, by jurors 3, 2, 1, laughing after jurors 2 and 1 finish their arguments. Jurors 8 and 9 join 2 and 1 in their arguments for guilty, and juror 7 listens intently to the discussion. Juror 5 continues to lead the not guilty group, by suggesting to them that they need to argue more for a not guilty verdict. Juror 7's responds to the calling and contributes his arguments to the discussion. Juror 9 interjects into the notguilty discussion and presents a counterpoint. Jurors 1 and 8 find holes in juror 9's argument, and say so; however, jurors 1 and 2, come to juror 9's rescue and they

119

support him in his arguments. Juror 2 helps 9, and jurors 1, 2, 8, 9 agree together. Once again, the guilty group is united and supportive of each other. Juror 5 continues to single-handedly argue for not guilty, and juror 9 continues to disagree. Jurors 2, 8 and 1 continue to support juror 9 in his arguments. Juror 5 appeals to juror 4, the foreperson, who is in legal studies, about his opinions and asks him questions. The answers do not help, since juror 5 continues to argue for not guilty. Juror 9 continues to argue and once more dominates the conversation, while jurors 8 and 1 agree with 9, and jurors 3 and 4 add to the argument and support the rest of the guilty group. Juror 8 addresses juror 7 directly, and asks for juror 7's opinion. This juror, who was previously not guilty hesitates, and responds guilty, but very quickly adds, that this should be a mistrial. Thus, it appears, that the guilty group, are starting to persuade some jurors as to their opinion. Juror 7 did not contribute much to the not guilty arguments, but it appears this juror has listened carefully and is changing his mind.

Jurors 2, and 9 are taking this opportunity to argue with juror 7 more, to convince him of the guilty verdict. Juror 5, however, interjects in this conversation, and presents his arguments for the not guilty verdict. Juror 3 responds to juror 5's arguments, and proceeds to argue with him. Juror 1 appears very eager and very quick to support juror 9, and along with juror 3 they support juror 9's arguments, and continue saying guilty.

Even though jurors 6 and 10 continue to support the not guilty verdict, they do not speak up and help juror 5 in arguing for their side. Juror 5 is fighting the battle by himself, and is doing it single-handedly. He is a very strong in this, since, even though he does not have much support, he does not waver in his convictions and beliefs. A whole

120

group is attacking him, but he restates his arguments and convictions, and does not appear to change his mind.

Juror 4 may be the foreperson, but it is juror 9 who clearly dominates, and leads the discussions. It could be said, however, that juror 9 and 5 are the strongest in the two groups, and lead their groups equally well. Juror 4, even though he has knowledge of the law, or so the group believes, remains in the background, and is happy to have others take the lead. The jurors are ready to have their final vote, and the guilty group has received two supporters. The split is 8 to 2.

Jurors 5 and 7 vote not guilty. Even though juror 7 was wavering, in the final vote he supports the leader of the not guilty group in his convictions. Juror 6, who has contributed nothing, to both the discussions, during the trial and deliberations, changes his mind and votes guilty. The story is similar with juror 10. This juror was more active during predeliberations discussions, but silent during deliberations. Even though the arguments were the same and restated all through the discussion, juror 10 became persuaded that the accused is guilty. Thus, the guilty group consists of jurors, 1, 2, 3, 4, 6, 8, 9, and 10. The lawyer's performance has not made much difference in the jurors' decision, with the exception of juror 5 who noted the defense lawyer trip over her words, and remembered this during the deliberations. He made reference to this.

Overall, however, the group who originally voted guilty stood together and supported one another in this. They were rarely in opposition with each other, and came to the rescue of their group members very quickly and eagerly. Juror 5 had strong opinions, and did not let himself be persuaded. No argument was going to change this juror's mind. His supporters were not as strong, and each one of them had doubts. Jurors

6 and 10 showed their doubts by crossing the line to join the other group, while juror 7 voiced his views out loud, and wavered between the two.

The foreperson was not a leader, and he had difficulties with deciding as to where he belonged. Very quickly he joined the stronger group, and sided with them. This leader did not direct the discussion, suggest votes, or make convincing arguments. It was juror 8 who took the most notes during the trial, and juror 9 who led the discussions. If juror 4 was studying another subject area, and was not in legal studies, he would not have been the group's choice for a leader.

Appendix E: Results for Condition 3

Defense Engaged, Crown Neutral.

As the trial is beginning, and all jurors take their seats. Jurors 6 through 10 are very attentive to the trial; juror 2 takes notes and juror 1 is looking around. As the trial progresses, two late individuals come in, however, they do not take the other jurors' attention from the trial. Juror 2 continues to take notes and the others pay attention to what is happening on the screen. Juror 8 laughs at the witness that is being examined, while juror 3 looks across at the other jury members and juror 1 takes of his jacket. A few minutes after the late jurors enter, Juror 5 becomes distracted by them. One of the persons who has arrived knows juror 5, and was trying to get his attention for a minute. Juror 5 is able to get back to the task at hand and continues to watch the trial. As this first segment of the trial comes to an end, most jurors have been attentive, and juror 2 was taking notes, all through the segment.

The first break begins, and the jurors have an opportunity to get to know one another. As the break begins, the group of 10 jurors divide themselves into pairs of two and have conversations within those small groups. Juror 4 talks with juror 5, while jurors 9 and 8 also enjoy a conversation among themselves. Juror 6 leaves the room, while juror 7 shuffles papers in front of himself. Juror 7 talks with juror 10, and jurors 9 and 8 join in and they enjoy a conversation together. Jurors 1 and 2 talk among themselves, and jurors 4 and 5 join in. Juror 3 listens to their conversation and smiles at first; however, after a few minutes juror 3 joins in the conversation of jurors 7, 8, and 10. Later, juror 6 joins in. This group conversation continues, but later they go back to the pairs. It is again juror 8 and 9 talking together, while jurors 1 and 2 listen, and 5 and 4 also talk among

123

themselves. Juror 9 engages juror 3 in conversation and they talk together for a few minutes. At the same time jurors 1 and 8 talk together and so do 6, 7 and 10.

Jurors 8 and 9 talk much among themselves; they are exchanging stories about school, and are the most engaged couple of the group. These two jurors have talked to each each other the most during this break. They are very comfortable together, and not only swap stories, but laugh together and seem to really get along. The other two pairs of jurors that talk much among themselves are jurors 4 and 5. Jurors 7 and 10 are having a nice talk among themselves. Juror 6 joins jurors 7 and 10 and they talk together. While juror 5 goes to get water, juror 4 starts talking with juror 8. Jurors 1 and 2 are the most unengaged and look uninterested, bored, and tired. Juror 1 puts his head on the table and tries to have a little nap.

After this first break, most of the conversations were about school, programs of study and professors. The conversations were mostly within small groups or pairs, but juror 8 was the most animated and showed leadership by engaging others in conversations. Juror 8 had most of his conversations with juror 9 and they seemed the most close. At the same time, jurors 1 and 2 were the most uninterested and unengaged.

The trial begins again, and the jurors turn their attention back to the trial. There is much action as this segment of the trial begins. Jurors 9 and 10 laugh after hearing the witness answer the lawyer's question. At the same time juror 7 has a paper and pen ready for note taking, but at the moment he is watching the trial intently and is not taking any notes yet. Juror 9 looks around, while juror 8 mouths "wow" in response to the witnesses testimony and the proclamation of death by the witness. Juror 9 smirks and juror 8 looks at 9 and smiles. All the other jurors are focused on the trial, and juror 2 continues to take notes, while juror 1 has his head on a table and looks to be asleep.

As the trial continues, most jurors are attentive, and juror 2 continues to take notes, while juror 3 looks at juror 2 once in a while. Juror 9 starts taking notes, and now it is both jurors 2 and 9 who are taking notes. Juror 1 wakes up and leans back to watch the trial. All members of the jury are giving the trial their full attention. Juror 9 continues to take notes, and silently communicates with juror 8. They exchange smiles before juror 9 returns to taking notes.

While the defense starts the cross examination, juror 9 continues to take notes and laughs at some of the responses. He is the only one. Juror 2 looks around and momentarily stops taking notes. Juror 2 goes back to taking notes. While the Crown calls a witness, jurors 9 and 2 are still taking notes. They are the only ones who take notes, but the others are attentive, and only juror 1 looks bored. Juror 9 started to get impatient at the end of the segment.

Another break has been announced and the jurors start talking again. During this segment of the trial, all jurors were attentive, but it was jurors 2 and 9 who took notes while paying attention the trial. Juror 1 continued to look tired and sleepy. As the break starts, all jurors stretch, and some yawn as well. Juror 4 asks a question of the group, but people are still yawning and no one responds. Juror 10 tries to make conversation, but everyone is still too busy stretching and yawning to response. Finally, juror 10 engages juror 7 in conversation and they talk together. Juror 8 asks a question of the group, and starts talking with jurors 2 and 9. Juror 9 tries to ask another general question of the group and this time juror 3 replies. Juror 3, however, is the only one who has responded

125

to juror 9's question, and since no one else replied, jurors 9, 10, and 8 started talking among themselves. This group of three jurors 8, 9 and 10 talk among themselves, especially juror 8. This juror does not stop. At the same time, jurors 1 and 2 are quiet, and do not contribute much to any conversation.

Juror 6 asks a question, and proceeds to talk to juror 10, while juror 3 is talking with juror 8. As the break continues, jurors 1 and 2 continue to be quiet and not talk with anyone, but jurors 8 and 9 talk to jurors 5, 4, and 3. During the break juror 7 was busy eating, and once he finished, he joined some conversations. Jurors 1 and 2 were mostly quiet, but on occasion they joined others and answered questions, or made a comment. Mostly though, these two jurors were quiet. While jurors 1 and 2 were quiet, jurors 8 and 9, and especially juror 8, were happily talking among themselves and with others. The break comes to an end and the jurors quiet down to start listening to the trial.

As the trial begins, juror 9 starts taking notes while jurors 2 and 1 put their heads on the desk, but still watch the trial. During the defense's first witness testimony, juror 2 doodles on the paper in front of him, while juror 9 continues to take notes. Juror 9 also shakes his head at the witness. At the same time, jurors 6 and 7 exchange glances and smiles, while juror 4 doodles on piece of paper and also looks antsy. During the defense's closing juror 2 looks very tired and bored. During this last segment of the trial, jurors 9 and 2 took the most notes. Other jurors were listening to the trial, but it was jurors 9 and 2 who took notes, and it was juror 9 who had the most reactions to the testimony.

The deliberations are about to begin. After the silent vote is over the jurors are ready to discuss the trial. Their first open vote is as follows: jurors 1, 3, 5, 6, 7, and 8, 9 vote guilty, while jurors 2 and 8 voted not guilty. Juror 4 was not sure, and did not decide on his vote at this time. The jurors were also ready to select a foreperson. Juror 9 asked

the group about who would like to have that role, and the group suggested that he could

be the foreperson. In the end, juror 9, who spoke first about the foreperson position,

becomes the foreperson. This individual does not seem to be in legal studies or have

experience being on a jury. This juror was also one of the most attentive jurors during the

trial and took the most notes. He also was one of the active jurors and it should be not

surprising that he was the leader and the foreperson in the end. It is also important to note

the vote split. At this point after the first open vote it is 7 jurors voting for a guilty verdict

and only 2 voting for a not guilty verdict, while one is undecided. This is important since,

by the end of the deliberation period, the jurors stand united in a not guilty verdict.

The deliberations begin, and it is juror 7 who speaks up first, and asks juror 2 why

he believes that the accused is guilty. Juror 2 replies that there is not enough evidence to

convict her. Jurors 9 and 8 laugh together at this and disagree. These two jurors had

similar opinions, and spent much time talking during the breaks in the trial, and at the

start of the deliberations they are supporting one another. Juror 7 does not gives up and

asks juror 8 about why he believes that the accused is guilty of first-degree murder.

Juror 8 presents arguments about the accused's deliberate motives, which in his eyes

makes her guilty of first-degree murder. Juror 7 speaks up and talks about the murder

being planned. This juror has voted guilty during the first vote, but of second-degree

murder. Juror 5 speaks up, but then juror 8 continues to talk about the murder being

planned, and presents a definition of what planned means in this case. Juror 2 presents

arguments and fleshes out the problems with the case. Thus far, only juror 2 is arguing for a not guilty verdict. Juror 7 agrees with juror 2 about some of the evidence not being as strong as it should have been.

Juror 10 speaks up, and asks about fingerprints. No one answers, though, but juror 2 continues to speak about the missing evidence that is making him vote not guilty. Juror 2 believes that if the murder happened closer to home he would be able to convict the accused, but since it happened so far, he cannot justify it to himself that it was the accused. Juror 9 speaks up and asks a question of the group about the amount of blood on the accused's shirt. Juror 2 speaks up and is surprised that the accused did not think of taking the shirt off, but kept it on, and got it all bloody, especially after the kitchen incident. Juror 7 starts to have doubts and says that it is not clear. To this, juror 2 speaks up and suggests that this is exactly the reason for which they should not convict her. Juror 10 makes a joke, and suggests that the accused, has taken the shirt off and it was her friend who put it on and committed the murder. No one is listening or laughing in response to this. Juror 9 is starting to have doubts, and not only finds another reason or a problem with the Crown's case, but now believes that this should be a mistrial. Juror 3 listens to most of the arguments so far, but he speaks up now and argues intent, but it is jurors 7 and 8 who argue against each other. Juror 5 speaks up and supports juror 8 in his stand. Juror 7, however, cuts juror 8 off and juror 2 supports juror 7 fully, since juror 7 was arguing for a not guilty verdict at this point. Juror 10 speaks up, but it is jurors 2 and 8 who argue together.

Juror 3 spoke up a few times, but mostly this juror was listening to others and smiling. Juror 9 asks a question, and both jurors 2 and 7 answer. These two jurors are in agreement, and juror 2 has found a supporter. Jurors 9, 8, 7, and 2 talk and juror 3 joins in. Juror 8 continues to disagree with jurors 2 and 7, but they continue to argue their points.

The jurors decide to take another vote. This time, all those who voted first-degree murder, changed their vote to at least second-degree. The split after the second vote is as follows: guilty of second-degree murder vote jurors 1, 3, 4, and 8. Not guilty vote jurors 2, 5, 6, 7, 9, and 10. Thus, after the second vote, the not guilty group are dominating, even though after the first vote it was the guilty group who had more supporters. The group continues to deliberate.

Juror 2 asks the group about who else could have committed the murder, but others start talking and they are not answering him. Juror 10 asks why second-degree murder and juror 1 presents arguments with which juror 10 does not agree, and continues to say that he needs more evidence for a conviction. Juror 1 and 10 continue to argue, but juror 10 is stronger in his arguments than juror 1. Juror 9 joins in the discussion, and so do jurors 2, 8, 3, and juror 9 and 10 are already arguing. The jurors who join in the discussion start poking holes in the Crown's case. Juror 7 takes control over the the discussion, while jurors 2, 8, 9, and 10 talk loudly. Juror 2 speaks up about the different variables that were not explained by the Crown. Juror 7 agrees, and makes a comment with which juror 10 agrees. Jurors 9 and 8 laugh as they hear the discussion and start speculating about how the defendant has committed the murder. Juror 2 brings the defendant's size up, and believes that the victim was much bigger than her, so she would not be able to inflict so many stab wounds. Juror 10 concludes that in a case where there is so many unanswered questions, this is just one more.

During most of the discussion jurors 4, 5, and 6 have not spoken and have been silent. Juror 5 finally makes a comment, but it is the same group who continues to argue the case. Jurors 2, 10, 8, 9, and 7 continue to argue and discuss the case. Juror 10 brings up other flaws. Juror 7 agrees, and speaks about all of the unanswered questions. Juror 2 also agrees with them. Juror 9 does agree that there are unclear points in the trial. Juror 10 agrees, and juror 2 brings up Jill, and to him she was a key player in the murder, but no one did anything about it or made a case against her. Jurors 6, 3, 4, and 5 are silent and do not contribute to the discussion.

After this discussion juror 8 is convinced and is willing to change his verdict. He says that he has been convinced and sees the case more clearly. Jurors 9, 2, and 8 continue talking about the case. The final vote occurs and all are in agreement that the verdict should be not guilty. During the deliberations, even though juror 9 was the foreperson, it was juror 2 who spoke up the most and made the most arguments. He was the juror who stood by his decision and convinced others that the not guilty verdict is the only verdict that should occur in this case. Juror 2 started in the minority, since only juror 10 was in agreement with him; however, after the deliberations were over, the other 7 jurors changed their vote. Juror 10 supported juror 2, but juror 2 was unquestioningly the most dominating voice. Jurors 3, 4, and 5 spoke the least, as did juror 6. Only here and there did these jurors make a comment, and they did not take a leading role in most of the discussions. It was mostly jurors 2, 8, 9, 10, and 7 who argued and discussed the case. Juror 1 was totally silent and was not heard at all. Thus, jurors 8 and 9 who spoke much during the trial, and juror 2 who was taking notes, were the key players during the deliberations.

Appendix F: Results for Condition 4

Crown Engaged, Defense Neutral.

As the trial begins all jurors are listening intently. Juror 7 is holding his head in his hands, and looking very intently at the screen. A few minutes into the trial, juror 5 starts to look around, and so does juror 7. At this point, other jurors also start to become restless. Juror 1 is playing with a pen and so is juror 3. Juror 4 nods at the screen while juror 6 moves in his seat. Juror 7 starts to yawn. All other jurors are still looking at the screen. As the first segment of the trial comes to an end, jurors look ready for a break. The first break arrives.

As the break begins, all jurors start to talk. It is jurors 3 and 7 who are having a conversation among themselves Following 3 and 7's example, 4 and 11 start talking and so are 1 and 5. Jurors 9 and 13 turn to one another and start talking as well. There are many pairs who are talking among themselves. Jurors 12, 6, 10, and 2 are laughing and talking together. Jurors 9 and 8 are talking to each other, and jurors 11and 4 who are talking together are joined by juror 8.

The only juror who does not seem to be talking is juror 7. The jurors are trying to get to know one another, and are using school as a common topic to learn about each other. They are all students, and are able to find school to be the common ground for all. Jurors 3 2, 11, and 4 are talking together while juror 7 is still not engaged in conversations with the other jurors. Juror 3 starts talking about midterms, and juror 8 joins him, and they talk about their test averages in Psychology 101. Juror 9 continues talking with juror 13, and jurors 10, 12, and 6 talk together.

Juror 7 continues to be bored, and puts his head on his hands; however, juror 3 engages him in conversations, and juror 7 starts talking with juror 3. While jurors 11, 4, and 8 are talking together, juror 2 is silent, and even though juror 7 looks tired and yawns, he is still talking with juror 3. Juror 3 engages juror 2 in a conversation. Most of the conversations are still in pairs, and jurors talk mostly with their neighbours and there is not much talk across the table. Juror 3 is talking with jurors 8 and 9, while juror 7 remains quiet. Juror 2 also looks tired and is not talking with anyone. Jurors 3, 4, and 8 are talking, and juror 11 is listening to them and smiling. Jurors 3 and 4 reengaging others in conversations, while jurors 7 and 2 are silent.

At the same time, jurors 1 and 5 are both talking and are very involved in their conversation, and so are jurors 9 and 13. They are enjoying their talk. Another pair that is talking animatedly are jurors 10 and 12. They only talk together and do not engage others. Juror 3 engages juror 7 and even though juror 2 is not contributing to their talk, juror 2 is listening, nodding and smiling at them. Jurors 11, 4 and 8 are quiet, but they listen intently to the conversation that jurors 3 and 7 are having together. Juror 2 finally joins jurors 3 and 7 in conversation, while jurors 11, 4, and 8 start talking among themselves.

During this break it was juror 3 who started many conversations with a variety of other jurors. This juror was most active and was trying to get to know others. At the same time, jurors 7, 2, 6 and 1 were fairly quiet, especially juror 7. This group of jurors enjoyed many small conversations with in pairs, rather than having small group discussions or large group talks. The same pairs talked through the break, and only a few jurors tried to engage others in conversations.

The break is over, however, and the jurors' attention is drawn back to the screen and the trial. As the trial begins, all jurors are listening intently. Juror 1 is doodling, but he is smiling at the screen and nodding, showing that he is listening. Juror 7 once again has his head in his hands, but is smiling and watching the screen. As the trial continues, all jurors are listening, and it is only juror 1 and 7 who are showing signs of boredom. Juror 1 is doodling all through the trial, while juror 7 yawns, rubs his eyes, and looks very tired.

The trial continues, and juror 1 instead of doodling is taking notes, while juror 10 is looking around, but he is not making eye contact with anyone. Juror 1 continues to take notes to the end of the trial segment, while juror 7 continues to look tired and yawns. Juror 8, at different parts of the trial, has leaned forward, and appeared to be looking and listening very intently to the lawyers' questioning of the witness. Juror 13 follows juror 8's example, and toward the end of the segment, leans forward and listens intently. During this segment of the trial, mostly juror 1 was active by taking notes as well as doodling, and juror 7 looked tired all through the segment. The other jurors listen to the trial, and mostly shifted in their seats and looked around the room, but showed no other signs of activity.

The second break is announced, and the jurors start talking. Similar to the first break, jurors 1 and 5 talk together, and so do jurors 9 and 13. These two pairs of jurors were involved in conversations during the first break, as well. The other jurors are listening to them and are slowly getting into conversations with others. Jurors 11, 4, and 8 start talking among themselves. The body language of juror 8 excludes juror 9, who is in conversation with juror 13, by having his back to juror 9. Jurors 6, 10, and 12 are talking together and laughing. Juror 2 listens to them, and is looking at this group, but does not join in, or contribute to the conversation.

As the break continues, juror 7 starts talking to juror 3 once again; these two jurors enjoyed talks before during the first break. While they are talking, juror 2 is listening and jurors 3 and 7 engage juror 2 in their conversation. Jurors 2 and 3 continue talking, while juror 7 starts listening to others, and looks around. This is not for long, since juror 3 engages juror 7 in conversation and turns his back on juror 2, who is out of the conversation.

During this break, the same people talked together as during the previous break.. Juror 7 also continued to look tired, and juror 2 did not speak much. Most of the jurors did not engage those across the table from them in conversations, but only talked to those next to them. There were many intense conversations, especially between jurors 11, 4 and 8. Even though they did not talk together, there were no uncomfortable silences, and jurors were working on getting to know one another. The trial was ready to start again, and all jurors turned their attention to the screen once more.

As the trial begins, juror 2 starts scratching his arm, and then proceeds to fluff his hair. Juror 1, at first leans on the desk and puts his chin in his hands, but than he starts taking notes, and not just playing with his pen. Juror 7 leans back at first and looks tired. This juror is observed looking at his watch, and playing with his sleeves. As the trial continues he starts paying closer attention, and leans forward to listen more intently. Juror 13 leans forward and imitates juror 1 at first, and then starts taking notes as well. As the trial draws to an end, all jurors are attentive, but there are small movements among them as they are awaiting the end of the trial. Many yawn, or shift in their seats. Juror 12 starts writing as the jurors receive instruction about the deliberations.

The trial is finally over, and all jurors stretch before they give their silent votes. When the jurors are ready to deliberate, juror 4 volunteers to be the foreperson, since no one else was eager to have the job. Unlike in the other conditions, this group of jurors do not take a vote, but go right in to discussing the trial, and juror 4 from the very beginning takes the lead, makes notes, and leads the discussions. This juror wants to get the job done as quickly and efficiently as possible. Juror 4 asks all jurors about the guilt of the accused and juror 10 responds, with which juror 6 agrees. Jurors 1, 5, and 8 all start talking, and juror 9 adds that the accused was drunk when the murder occurred. At the same time jurors 12, 13, and 1 discuss the crime and want to make sure first that the crime was actually possible for the accused to have committed. Juror 12 does not think that the crime was possible, or rather, that the accused was able to have committed it. Juror 5 picks up the intoxication point, and juror 1 disagrees. This juror does not believe that the accused was drunk. Juror 4 responds to the intoxication point, but juror 12 continues to talk about the possibility of the accused being able to stab the victim. He does not think that it was possible, and juror 5 disagrees with that.

Juror 4 steers the conversation to the blood found on the accused's shirt, and the splatter found by the police. Juror 3 and 9 make a comment about that. Juror 4 then brings up the knife and jurors 12, 9, and 4 move on to discuss the knife, with which the accused stabbed the victim. Juror 4 continues to bring important points up, such as the cheating. Juror 5 makes a comment and juror 10 joins in this discussion about cheating of the victim on the accused with a girl by the name of Jill. Jurors 11 and 2 speak up, and juror 13 brings in the reaction of the accused to the news that her boyfriend was murdered. Jurors 12, 3, and 9 comment on the reaction of the accused, and her lack of emotion to the news.

All jurors look very involved in the discussion, and are taking it very seriously. Juror 3 goes back to the knife and talks about her ideas out loud. Juror 4 picks up that point and starts discussing the blood once again. Juror 3 joins the conversation and replies to juror 4's statements, and juror 4 continues to talk about the blood. Juror 10 agrees with juror 4 and so does juror 9, who is defending juror 4 against juror 12 who disagrees with juror 4's statements and reasoning.

At this point juror 12 is the only one who is arguing not guilty. All other jurors are bringing up points for a guilty verdict. Jurors 4, 5, 10, 6, 12 and 1 are all involved in a discussion of the accused's guilt and the blood that was found on the accused's shirt. Juror 12 moves on to talk about the accused's behavior the day after the murder, and comments on the accused being in her room most of the day and longer. Jurors 1 and 10 join the discussion, but juror 12 continues to brings up points, such as being stabbed in the back, and talking about how that can be realistic. Juror 13 comments that there is not enough evidence to prove beyond the shadow of the doubt that the accused is guilty, with which jurors 3 and 10 agree.

Juror 10 starts talking about the blood and wounds that the victim received, and argues for a not guilty verdict. Juror 1 starts talking against the not guilty verdict and 12 disagrees, and brings up the knife again. Jurors 6, 11, and 4 join in, and they continue to discuss the blood, as well as premeditation. Juror 4 takes a lead, and starts to review the evidence that they know. As juror 4 reviews the evidence, jurors 3 and 12 disagree with some of the evidence that juror 4 has presented to them. Juror 10 argues for the not guilty verdict, by making comments about the accused being able to find the victim in the park. Juror 4 does not give up and continues to review evidence for a guilty verdict. Juror 12 picks up where juror 4 has left of and speaks about the details of the case. Jurors 3 and 6 disagree with juror 12's remarks. Juror 7 joins in, and brings more points that would make the accused guilty.

Juror 4 takes charge, and asks for a list of evidence that would make the accused not guilty. Juror 11 responds, and gives juror 4 reasons for the accused being not guilty. Juror 12, joins juror 11, and remarks that the accused would have had a hard time finding the victim in the park. Juror 7 however, does not give up, and speaks up against 11 and 12. Juror 7 believes that the accused knew the pattern of behavior of the victim and had no problems finding him in the park. Jurors 12 and 10 disagree with juror 7 and start arguing for a not guilty verdict. Juror 6 joins in, and makes a comment on the length of the accused and victim's relationship. Juror 4 continues to believe that the accused is guilty. Jurors 12 and 6 talk about the accused's history of violence and that there was none. They believe that the roommate of the victim did not like her and made her look worse than the accused deserved.

At this point all the jurors join the conversation and all are arguing at once. Juror 10 suggest that they have a vote, but juror 13 exclaims loudly that all the evidence points to a not guilty verdict. Juror 9 agrees with juror 13, and juror 6 disagrees. It is the foreperson who steps in and talks about the evidence and how important that is to their decision. Juror 5 speaks up and agrees with juror 13 that there is not enough to convict the accused. Jurors 10, 8, and 1 join in and start questioning the knife. Juror 1 is talking, and jurors 9, 10, and 12 all agree with 1 and add to his arguments. Juror 4 steps in again, and lists the evidence that they have. Jurors 12 and 10 disagree with juror 4 and the evidence that he is presenting to the group. Juror 6 steps in and starts disagreeing with jurors 12 and 10. He believes that the accused and the victim had to have met somewhere that night. Juror 1 joins in and agrees that the accused had to be there, since the pattern of blood points to that. Juror 10 agrees with that and juror 4 continues to list the evidence that points to a guilty verdict. Juror 13 continues to have problems with the knife and says so.

Juror 4, while listing all that they know, says that all the evidence points to a guilty verdict. Jurors 10 and 12 disagree. Juror 7 supports jurors 10 and 12, while juror 6 speaks up for a guilty verdict. Jurors 4 and 12 argue together about the blood on the accused's shirt, and the expert's testimony. Jurors 1 and 5 talk about guilt and the amount of alcohol that the accused had to drink that night. Juror 4 wants to vote and make a final decision.

The group votes, and the first open vote shows the following results: jurors 9, 10, 11, and 12 vote not guilty, while jurors 1, 2, 3, 4, 5, 6, 7, 8, and 13 vote guilty of second-degree murder. Juror 3 brings up guilt once again, and juror 10 believes that there is not enough evidence to convict. Juror 4 disagrees with this fully. Juror 11 joins in and argues for a not guilty verdict alongside juror 10. Juror 6 joins in, and starts to argue against jurors 10 and 11. Juror 7 joins in to support juror 6. Juror 3 joins in, and does his best to support jurors 6 and 7, by talking about the blood splatter analysis. Juror 10 is not convinced and juror 11 wants more evidence. Juror 6 does not give up and continues to argue for guilty, by explaining to jurors 10 and 11 that the lack of evidence is normal, and if that was not the case trials would not happen, since everything is not crystal clear. Juror 5 joins in and is supporting juror 6. At the same time jurors 9 and 4 are talking together, and juror 4 is refuting all the arguments that juror 9 is making for the not guilty group. Juror 10 does not give up, and claims that important evidence is missing. Juror 7 challenges that, and asks juror 10 about the important missing evidence.

At this point all jurors are talking at once about the dumpster in which the evidence was found. Jurors 10, 11 and 12 are still not convinced that the accused is guilty. Juror 10 is weakening, since he is asking the group for the appeal process. Juror 4 tries to argue the guilty points again, and juror 12 makes a point about assumptions when it comes to the blood that was found. All jurors that are voting guilty jump on juror 12. Juror 10 feels the pressure, and says that he will vote guilty even though he does not believe in that verdict.

Juror 12 continues to argue not guilty, but now juror 10 is attacking him, and is arguing for the guilty side. It is interesting, that this juror has changed so quickly. There is a change of opinions at this point. Juror 3 now is saying that the accused is not guilty, while juror 9 is saying guilty and so is juror 12, who was fighting for a not guilty verdict. Juror 11, who also was voting not guilty is now changing his mind and voting guilty, while 13 says that the accused is not guilty. Juror 13 is under a lot of pressure from the others to change his vote.

Juror 10 now is arguing very strongly for a guilty verdict, and is doing everything in his power to convince juror 13 that the accused is guilty. This is very interesting, since juror 10 was such a strong supporter of not guilty, however, as soon as he changed his mind, he is arguing stronger than any other guilty supporter for that side. Jurors 4, 5, 7, and 10 are now all trying to persuade juror 13's mind, since at this point he is the only one who is still holding on to not guilty. This juror was on the guilty side for a while, but now is holding very strongly to the not guilty verdict. Juror 4 takes a lead, and tells juror 13 not to feel pressured, however, he will review all the evidence once more, and maybe juror 13 will see the reasoning behind the guilty verdict. Juror 4 proceeds to do so, and in the end juror 13 changes his mind, so the jurors come to a collective decision of guilty of second-degree murder.

During the end of the deliberations juror 10 changed his mind, even though for a long time he did not believe in that decision. Similarly, juror 13 voted guilty, but did not look convinced. By the expression on his face, one can deduce that it was the pressure from the rest of the group, especially the leader, that made this juror change is mind or just vote guilty with the others to end this session.

During this trial, once again, jurors spoke more within pairs during the breaks than in small groups, and no leader emerged during those discussions. During the deliberations, however, juror 4 became the leader, and acted as one throughout the deliberations. His manner, and listing his own convictions, helped him to persuade the other jurors. He was very well organized, and his points were strong. He was also one of the dominate voices during the deliberations. In the end, jurors who less strong, and did not have support of their opinions in others voted guilty more from pressure than actual conviction, especially juror 13. Thus, pressure from the group was an important factor in this verdict.

Lightning Source UK Ltd.
Milton Keynes UK
UKOW041119091011

180027UK00004B/1/P